MILLENNIAL MAJORITY

Morley Winograd & Michael D. Hais

San Francisco

Published by Blue Zephyr
Copyright © 2015 by Mike and Morley, LLC

All rights reserved

No part of this book may be reproduced or utilized in any form or by any means, electronic or mechanical, or by any information storage and retrieval system, without written permission from the publisher. The only exception to this prohibition is "fair use" as defined by U.S. copyright law.

www.mikeandmorley.com

ISBN-13: 978-1517063580
ISBN-10: 1517063582

MILLENNIAL MAJORITY

How a New Coalition Is Remaking American Politics

CONTENTS

Introduction 1

Chapter One: New Party Coalitions for a New Century 3

Chapter Two: Changing the Country's Civic Ethos for the Fourth Time 15

Chapter Three: Remaking the Grand Old Party 21

Chapter Four: Will the Democrats Keep On, Keepin' On? 39

Chapter Five: Reconstructing Obama's Presidential Opportunity 53

Chapter Six: Embracing a Millennial Era Civic Ethos 69

Conclusion 85

Epilogue 89

References 99

INTRODUCTION

Over the last five years, nearly all of the predictions we made in our two books about the impact of the Millennial generation on American politics and public policy have come true.

Our first book, <u>Millennial Makeover: MySpace, YouTube and the Future of American Politics,</u> written in 2007 and published in 2008, predicted that year's presidential campaign would result in the election of someone like Barack Obama and the realignment of partisan preferences leading to Democratic dominance at the presidential level for the following forty years.

Our second book, <u>Millennial Momentum: How a New Generation is Remaking America,</u> examined the impact of generational change on the fundamental civic ethos of the country and predicted that a new coalition, with Millennials at its heart, would allow President Obama to win the debate over the size and scope of government in the 2012 election.

The same data-driven insights and focus on generational change that allowed us to accurately foresee these results makes it possible for us to outline the future of America's politics and public policy over the next few decades. This book is designed to do just that.

America is in now in the middle of a period of great political tension and debate. That conflict will be resolved with the establishment of a new consensus about the role of the federal government that will be as powerful, distinctive, and long-lasting as the New Deal. The Democratic Party enters the debate with a strategic demographic advantage thanks to strong support from its coalition of Millennials, ethnic and racial minorities and women. But, the Democratic Party's ultimate success will be heavily dependent on not just the policies and performance of Barack Obama in his second term, but the political and communications skills of the President. For the Republican Party to be a serious contender in this debate, it will need to completely rethink how to reshape its message of individual liberty and responsibility for a new generation and a more diverse nation.

Regardless of which party is successful, history suggests that the final consensus on America's civic ethos will emerge after a continued period of struggle over the next decade that will test the mettle of every player on the current political scene and some who have not yet entered the fray. This book describes the parameters of that struggle, its likely outcome, and what American politics, government and public policy will look like during the next four decades in a nation shaped by the emerging Millennial generation.

CHAPTER ONE:
NEW PARTY COALITIONS FOR A NEW CESNTURY

In many democracies, political parties represent particular interests: labor or business, specific religions, ethnicities, or regions. In the United States, with its continental dimensions, varied population and economy, and a constitutional system designed to disperse governing power, political parties are historically, and still remain, coalitions of various societal groups. No party completely monopolizes the members of any one demographic, and each party contains at least some representation from all segments of the population. But, at any time, each party's coalition is centered on a particular set of groups that underpin its electoral support and shape its policy agenda.

The party coalitions are impermanent. They are formed in a nation with a constantly changing economy, political process, and demographic makeup and they change along with, and as a result of, the transformations in the society of which they are a part. As Sean Trende correctly points out in his book, The Lost Majority, there is always some movement in the composition of the party coalitions from one election to the next.

However, because most Americans identify with a political party and because, once formed, their party identification does not change during their lifetime, major changes in the composition of the party coalitions are rare. Once formed, party coalitions have staying power that keeps them largely intact for decades, certainly well beyond a single election or two.

Nevertheless, party coalitions have changed significantly in the course of American history due to the coming of age of new generations and large scale changes in the demographic composition of the electorate. These changes have disrupted the balance between the parties and the direction of public policy. Starting with V. O. Key in the mid-1950s, political scientists have referred to these massive coalitional changes and the electoral and policy transformations that they produce as "realignments."

While some observers, such as Trende and political scientist David Mayhew, raise doubt about the existence of realignments or the usefulness of the concept in describing the course of American politics, massive incidences of electoral and political change have clearly taken place throughout U.S. history. These eras of change or, in fact, realignments, have occurred with almost clockwork precision about every forty years, making them too obvious to ignore or attribute their occurrence simply to chance.

One Hundred Fifty Years of Alternating Party Coalition Change and Stability

At the time of the Civil War, the newly formed Republican Party built a majority coalition based on mercantile New England, the industrial Middle Atlantic, the agricultural Midwest, and the newly admitted Western states. Poised against this Republican coalition was a Democratic coalition centered primarily on the states of the Southern Confederacy. In the middle, both geographically and electorally, were the Border States—Maryland, Delaware, Kentucky, West Virginia and occasionally New Jersey and Indiana—the battleground states of the era whose votes often determined the outcome of presidential elections.

While those elections were often very close with less than a percentage point separating the Democratic and Republican nominees and partisan control of one or both Congressional houses shifting on a fairly regular basis, the GOP did win 7 of the 9 presidential elections from 1860-1892. As a result, public policy during this period reflected the Republican Party's beliefs in federal government action to stimulate industrial and agricultural growth in an expanding nation.

However, the transformation of the nation's economy by the Industrial Revolution resulted in conflicts between industrial interests, rural America, and the emerging urban working class.

The result was a political realignment that extended the GOP's electoral dominance, but with completely different party coalitions facing off against one another. In the hotly contested election of 1896, the Republican nominee, William McKinley, representing the interests of newly powerful industrialists handily defeated Democrat William Jennings Bryan, who defended the fading economic power and cultural significance of farmers in his famous "Cross of Gold" convention speech. Once again, the Republican Party won 7 of the next 9 presidential elections, losing only when splits within the majority GOP enabled Democrat Woodrow Wilson to win in 1912 and 1916. Unlike the previous era, however, the Republican margins were usually large and generally increased throughout the era.

Initially, the Republican coalition consisted of New England, the Middle Atlantic States, and the more established agricultural states east of the Missouri River. It was opposed by a coalition that contained the traditionally Democratic South and the newer agricultural and mining states of the West. By the 1920s, when William Jennings Bryan, a candidate with particular appeal in the Prairie and Rocky Mountain region, was no longer on the scene, only the former Confederate States were regularly Democratic. This Republican electoral strength produced public policy that ratified the laissez faire economic beliefs of the commercial and industrial interests that dominated the GOP of that era, best summarized by President Coolidge's pronouncement that "the business of America is business."

Seven decades of Republican hegemony finally ended with the Great Depression. Beginning with his first election in 1932, Franklin Roosevelt began to assemble the New Deal coalition comprised of the Southern Whites who had provided the core of the Democratic vote in previous eras; the GI or "Greatest Generation" children of eastern and southern European immigrants; white workers across the country; and, blacks in the big cities of the North. This coalition dominated U.S. electoral politics for four decades, winning seven of nine presidential elections between 1932 and 1964. It also restructured public policy domestically, transforming the nation's economic structure from laissez faire to governmental activism; and internationally, moving the nation's foreign policy from isolationism to interventionism.

Dominant and determinative as the New Deal coalition was in its time, its strength and influence eventually waned. New generations with new concerns emerged in the midst of the racial and lifestyle changes of the 1960s and the Democratic coalition assembled by Roosevelt fell apart, just as the prevailing GOP coalition of the late 19th and early 20th centuries had before it. The New Deal coalition was supplanted by a Republican coalition that increasingly added two former components of the older Democratic alignment—the white South and working-class whites—to the upper income white residents of suburbs and small towns outside of the South that had been the core of the GOP vote in the previous era.

The new Republican coalition dominated national elections, winning seven of ten presidential elections between 1968 and 2004, and shaped public policy almost as profoundly as the New Deal coalition it replaced. If the social and economic initiatives of FDR's New Deal, JFK's New Frontier, and LBJ's Great Society were not completely eradicated, they were sharply curtailed and rarely expanded. The one successful Democratic president of this Republican age, Bill Clinton, fully recognized that he was operating in a different time when he famously declared in his 1996 State of the Union address that "the era of big government is over."

Demographic Transformation Produces New 21st Century Party Coalitions

And now, as in the 1860s, 1890s, 1930s, and 1960s, the party coalitions are once again changing on a large scale. At the core of these changes are a number of demographic, economic, and societal transformations that are making America a very different country than it has been at any other time in its history.

• The Emergence of the Millennial Generation. The Millennial Generation, born 1982-2003, is the largest in U.S. history. There are 95 million Millennials, displacing Baby Boomers as the nation's largest generation by a margin of ten million people. By 2020, Millennials will comprise more than one-third of the national electorate. Millennials like their GI, or Greatest Generation, great grandparents before them are a group-oriented type of generation, labeled "civic" by generational theorists. As the GI Generation did, Millennials tend to favor activist government in economic matters and multilateralism in foreign affairs as well as tolerance on social and ethnic issues. As a result, the Millennial Generation is the first since the GI Generation in which a plurality self-identify as liberal rather than conservative.

• Increased Ethnic and Religious Diversity. In the late 1960s, when the GOP became the country's dominant political party, about ninety-percent of Americans were both white and Christian and two-thirds were Protestant. Most nonwhites were African-American. There were so few Hispanics or Asians that the Census Bureau did yet have separate racial designations for those groups. Today, the number of white Americans has declined to slightly less than seven in ten while the number of Hispanics has risen to around 15 percent and Asians to five-percent. African-Americans are about 10-percent of the population, as they have been since at least the turn of the 20th Century. The percentage of Americans who are Christian has fallen to about three-quarters and, in 2012, for the first time ever, less than half of the nation's adults are Protestant. By contrast, the number of adherents to non-Christian faiths and those affiliated with no religion has at least doubled.

America is expected to become even more ethnically and religiously diverse in the coming decades. For the first time ever, a majority of children being born in the U.S. are nonwhite. By no later than 2050, America is projected to be a "majority-minority" country,(one in which there will be more nonwhites than whites). Much of this change is being driven by the Millennial Generation, the most ethnically diverse in the nation's history. About forty-percent of Millennials are nonwhite; one in five have at least one immigrant parent; barely half are Christian; and three-in-ten profess no religious affiliation.

• The Rise of Women. In 1920, the 19th Amendment guaranteed women the right to vote. But, for almost the following six decades, because more traditionally-minded women were hesitant to exercise the suffrage, men continued to account for a majority of those voting for president for the following six decades. However, at least since the mid-1980s, women have voted at a higher rate than men and in both 2008 and 2012 women contributed a clear majority (53%) of the presidential electorate. During the past half century, women have caught, and often passed, men in other arenas as well. At the turn of the 20th Century, only a minuscule six percent of married women and less than half of single women (44%) worked for pay outside the home. By the turn of the next century, employment for pay among married women had risen to 60 percent and among single women to 69 percent. By 2010 women comprised a majority (54%) of the nation's workforce as well as its electorate. Women are also outpacing men in America's classrooms. Starting as far back as the 1940s, women have been as likely to attend high school as men. By 1968, a substantially greater percentage of women than men graduated from high school (75% to 68%). More recently, especially among Millennials, the ever-widening educational achievement gap between the sexes has clearly moved to higher education. In 2006, about 58 percent of college students were women. That year, women earned 63 percent of associate's degrees, 58 percent of bachelor's degrees, 60 percent of master's degrees, and 49 percent of doctorates awarded in the United States. By 2016, women are projected to earn 64 percent of associate's degrees, 60 percent of bachelor's degrees, 63 percent of master's degrees, and 56 percent of doctorates. All of this means that American women are less reliant on men for their economic sustenance and more likely to independently determine their political beliefs, identifications, and behavior than at any previous time in history.

• Mass Education Becomes a Reality. Although women may have taken better advantage of the change, the entire U.S. population has benefited from a large scale increase in educational achievement over the past century. As recently as 1940, three-quarters of American adults had not completed high school while just five percent had graduated from college. By 2012, 57 percent had either graduated from high school or had some college experience and almost a third (31%) had earned at least one college degree.

• The Decline of the White Working Class. The rise in educational attainment was accompanied by an equally profound change in the occupational composition of the U.S. workforce, especially among white Americans. In 1940, according to the calculations of Ruy Texiera and Alan Abramowitz, 58 percent of employed whites were "working class" (manual workers or farmers). By 2006, that number had fallen to 25 percent. Together, these massive demographic changes have transformed the two party coalitions, just as such alterations have done on four previous occasions during the past century and a half. This time, however, unlike during the last transformative period in the 1960s and 1970s, it is the Democratic Party rather than the GOP that is the beneficiary of demographic transformation in America.

The 21st Century Party Coalitions Coalesce

The past two decades have been marked by resurgence in the fortunes of the national Democratic Party, at least at the presidential level. The Democrats have won the popular vote in five of the last six presidential elections, beginning with Bill Clinton's victory in 1992. In 2012, Barack Obama became only the third Democrat ever to win a popular vote majority in successive elections. The previous two were the transformative presidential giants, Andrew Jackson (1828 and 1832) and Franklin Roosevelt (1932, 1936, 1940, and 1944). It is a distinction that eluded successful Democratic presidents such as Wilson, Truman, Kennedy, Johnson, and Clinton.

President Obama also won reelection with the nation's unemployment level at 7.9 percent, the highest level at which a president had been reelected since Franklin Roosevelt's landslide 1936 victory in the midst of the Great Depression, when unemployment stood at nearly 17 percent. Indeed, no president since FDR had won reelection when unemployment was above 7.2 percent.

Obama and Roosevelt have a number of other important things in common. Both were well liked personally. Both advocated a new formulation of the nation's civic ethos or understanding of the scope and purpose of government that was supported by most voters. Both also presided over and took advantage of a massive reformation of the party coalitions, something that seemed to obviate the old political rules of thumb.

Barack Obama's reelection win over Mitt Romney in 2012 was decisive—four percentage points, nearly five million popular votes and an electoral vote margin of 332 to 206. Although Obama's victory was ultimately clear-cut, it did not seem certain in the run up to the election to many inside-the-Beltway observers. The pundits' perceptions that economics would override the loyalty to the president and his party of the new components of the Democratic coalition was reinforced by polls showing core Democratic groups—Millennials, Hispanics, African-Americans, and women—less interested in the campaign and not as concerned about the election's outcome as core GOP groups—seniors, men, and whites. Millennial disenchantment with Obama and lack of interest in the election was a particular concern. Right up to Election Day Republicans and conservatives, believed this "enthusiasm gap" would propel Mitt Romney to the White House. The Romney campaign even "skewed" its polls to reflect a maximum turnout of those voting for its candidate and a minimal turnout of those inclined toward Obama based on this difference in enthusiasm.

In the end, the key component groups within the emerging Democratic coalition ended up voting at rates equivalent to, if not greater than, their turnout in Barack Obama's 2008 victory. Once at the polls, the members of those groups supported the president's reelection by large margins. Solid majorities of women (55%), 18-29 year old Millennials (60%), African-Americans (93%), Hispanics (71%), Asian-Americans (73%), Jews (69%), those who do not affiliate with any religious faith (70%), and unmarried persons (62%) voted for Barack Obama. By contrast, a majority of men (52%), seniors (56%), whites (59%), Protestants (59%), and married persons (56%) cast ballots for Mitt Romney.

Drilling down into the data, differences among more granularly-defined groups become even sharper. White men preferred Romney over Obama by 65 percent to 35 percent, while African-American and Latino women voted for Obama over Romney by even larger margins (96% to 3% among the former and 76% to 23% among the latter). White Protestants (69% to 30%) and white Catholics (59% to 40%) voted overwhelmingly for Romney, while whites with no religious affiliation favored Obama 63 percent to 31 percent. Non-whites of all faiths voted for Obama by a margin of greater than four-to-one (80% to 18%). Married men preferred Romney over Obama by 60 percent to 38 percent, while unmarried women voted for Obama against Romney by 67 percent to 31 percent.

In the end, the majority Democratic coalition, based most heavily on the Millennial generation, nonwhites, women, especially single women, the Northeast and the West, came together to defeat a smaller Republican coalition built on men, whites, especially those in the working and lower middle classes, seniors, and much of the South and Rocky Mountain west. If anything, Obama's slightly more narrow 2012 victory was even more dependent on the new Democratic coalition than his 2008 win had been. While support for the president declined between 2008 and 2012 among men, whites and those over 45, it remained constant or even rose among women, African-Americans, Hispanics, Asians, and the youngest voters.

Because Millennials and Hispanics are still increasing their contribution to the electorate, both were particularly crucial in 2012 and will be in the years ahead. CIRCLE, a non-partisan organization that researches and strives to increase youthful civic participation, analyzed exit polls and found that without solid Millennial support in Florida (66% of young people voted for Obama), Pennsylvania (63%), Ohio (62%), and Virginia (61%), the president would not have carried those battleground states and been reelected. Meanwhile, numerous post-election articles described the devastating impact of Mitt Romney's and the GOP's abysmal performance among Hispanics and the need for it to do much better with this emerging force in the future.

Will the 21st Century Party Coalitions Have Staying Power?

In 1948, the Republican Party was confident of victory. The charismatic Franklin Delano Roosevelt, with his mesmerizing radio voice, had been dead for three years. His successor, the far less charming Harry Truman, seemed much easier to defeat than FDR had been. Similarly, in 1988, Ronald Reagan, the "Great Communicator," was about to leave the presidency. When his vice-president, the less comfortable and somewhat stilted, George H. W. Bush, won the Republican presidential nomination, Democrats saw an opportunity to win back the White House. In both 1948 and 1988, however, the challenging party was disappointed.

Today, at least some Republicans believe that a more traditional

Democratic presidential nominee will be easier to defeat in 2016 than the African-American, Barack Obama, with his "rock star" personal appeal to blacks, Hispanics, and Millennials. But, there is considerable evidence to suggest that the emerging 21st Century Democratic coalition is likely to persist and even gather strength after Barack Obama leaves the presidency.

First, the Democratic coalition began to come together well in advance of Barack Obama's emergence onto the national political stage. The gender gap separating the political attitudes and voting preferences of women and men first emerged with the election of Ronald Reagan in 1980. From that time on, women have consistently been more "liberal" on most political issues and more likely to vote for Democrats than have men. Furthermore, a majority of the first segment of Millennials to vote for president cast ballots for John Kerry over George W. Bush in 2004, three years before Obama announced that he was running for president.

In addition, solid majorities of African-Americans and Hispanics have voted Democratic for decades. Never have fewer than 82 percent of African-Americans voted Democratic for president since the 1960s, when the GOP first nominated Barry Goldwater, who had voted against the 1964 Civil Rights Act guaranteeing blacks access to public accommodations, and then Richard Nixon and his successors won the presidency with a "Southern Strategy" of veiled racial appeals. Since 1972, the presidential vote for Democrats of Hispanics has averaged 64 percent, falling below that level to 53 percent only in 2004, when George W. Bush and Karl Rove specifically targeted Latinos.

Finally, the key component groups of each party's 21st Century coalitions clearly identify themselves as either Democrats or Republicans, an attachment that is far deeper and longer lasting than a vote for a specific candidate in a particular election. The concept of party identification was first described in the 1950s by four social scientists affiliated with the University of Michigan in their seminal book, The American Voter. Based on national surveys, the authors reported that upward of nine in ten American adults identified with or leaned to one of the major political parties. For the large majority, this psychological attachment to a party was formed when one was a young adult and remained constant throughout the remainder of their life. Nearly six decades later, in a replication of the original research, The American Voter Revisited, a new group of social scientists used a panel of survey respondents interviewed at four different points in time over a seventeen-year period (1965-1982) to once again clearly demonstrate the long-term stability of party identification. A large majority of Americans—more than eight in ten—identified with or leaned to one of the parties and upward of eight in ten of party identifiers affiliated with the same party at the end of the period that they did at the beginning. More recently, in the presidential election years of 2000 and 2004, a similar panel showed an equivalent level of willingness to identify with a party and stability in that identification over time. Extensive national surveys conducted by the communications research and consultation firm, Frank N. Magid Associates, in 2010 and replicated two years later, described the parameters and composition of the two current party coalitions based on those who identify with each of the parties. In August 2012, a majority of voters who identified with or leaned to the Republican Party were males (54%) and members of America's two oldest generations—Baby Boomers (those in their 50s to mid-60s) and those in the Silent Generation or seniors—who together made up 53 percent of Republicans. The GOP coalition was almost entirely white (81%) and disproportionately southern (38% of all Republicans and 41% of strong Republican identifiers). Forty percent of Republicans resided in small towns and rural areas. Three-quarters were Christian; only seven percent were unaffiliated with any faith. A third of all GOP identifiers and 42 percent of strong Republicans attended religious services at least once a week.

The coalition of Democratic identifiers was much different. A majority (53%) were women and from the country's two youngest generations—Millennials (voters 18-30) and Generation X (31-47 year olds), who in total made up 57 percent of Democrats. Forty-one percent of all Democrats and 45 percent of strong Democrats were nonwhite with about equal numbers of African-Americans and Hispanics. Nearly half of the Democratic identifiers lived in the Northeast and West, and a disproportionately large number—70 percent—lived in big cities or suburbs. Just half were married. Only 57 percent were Christian, and about one in five were either of non-Christian denominations or unaffiliated with any faith. Just

21 percent of Democratic identifiers attended a religious service weekly. Slightly more (24%) never did.

Over the past decade a new set of party coalitions has clearly emerged in America and, during the presidency of Barack Obama, has begun to solidify. The Democratic Party, with its coalition built on rising demographics—Millennials, minorities, and women—appears to have an electoral edge over the GOP with its coalition based on declining population segments—seniors, whites, and men. These partisan coalitional lines are likely to stand until party coalitions shift again under the stress and strain of demographic and generational change, probably at some point in the middle of the 21st century. In the meantime, the two parties will have to determine the strategies and tactics that will enable them to compete electorally and contribute most effectively to the process of governance in the Millennial era that is just beginning.

CHAPTER TWO:
CHANGING THE COUNTRY'S CIVIC ETHOS
FOR THE FOURTH TIME

Changes in political party coalitions have enormous consequences in the direction that the country takes in determining its public policies. Changes in public policy flow directly from the shifts in political coalitions that become evident in realigning elections every forty years or so. But about every eighty years, the emergence in the electorate of a "civic" generation, of which Millennials are the most recent, forces the country not just to change its public policies but to reassess the existing consensus on the proper role and scope of function of government. These landmark elections determine the answer to this question by redefining the nation's civic ethos, and the consensus that forms as a result of these historical contests lasts for four or five decades.

Both Barack Obama and Mitt Romney certainly seemed to have recognized that the 2012 election would play such a crucial role in the nation's history. At various points during the campaign, the president clearly expressed his beliefs about what he believed America's civic ethos should be. He said that he expected the 2012 election to be one "between Republicans who don't believe in government as a partner with the private sector and Democrats who do." At another time, he observed that, "There is a thread running through our history, a belief that through government, we should do together what we cannot do as well for ourselves." His campaign's voter turnout messages also made it clear that nothing less than the future civic ethos of the country was at stake in the outcome of the 2012 election.

Romney agreed on the critical nature of the 2012 campaign, but he had a different viewpoint on the role of government. He compared his perspective on that question directly with his interpretation of the president's in a similar effort to motivate his supporters to vote. "Obama's fundamental error is that he believes government creates jobs and opportunity. He is wrong. He puts his faith in government. I put my faith in people...We are only inches away from no longer being a free economy, this election could be our last chance."

The history of generational change in America suggests that there is no such thing as last chances in American politics, only temporary victories and defeats. However, both candidates were right to underline the historical significance of the 2012 election in creating a new civic ethos for the nation.

Turnings in Time

In their second book, The Fourth Turning, the founders of generational theory, William Strauss and Neil Howe, described the sequence of events that have engulfed the nation's political life when a young "civic" generation enters adulthood and begins to make its presence felt in the electorate. The Millennial Generation is the latest generation of that civic archetype to stir up a major debate about the nature and role of government in American life. The almost 250 year-long historical trail of disruptions of the existing order and the establishment of a new civic ethos provides critical clues as to where the nation is on the path it has embarked upon in the 21st century and how the journey is likely to turn out.

The Boston Tea Party in 1773, the election of the new Republican Party's presidential candidate, Abraham Lincoln in 1860, the stock market crash of 1929, and the financial collapse that brought about the Great Recession in September of 2008 are generally recognized as the catalytic events that began the previous four "fourth turnings," to use the name Strauss and Howe gave to these crucial moments, which have altered the course of American history. These events have an outsized impact on the political attitudes of the youngest adult generation at the time. The catalytic event provides the young generation the impetus to become engaged in civic life and to demand changes in the existing structures of government.

As a result, catalytic events set off a fierce debate about what the nation's new civic ethos should be. The battle of Lexington and

Concord in 1775 inspired those favoring the cause of independence from the British to reconvene the Continental Congress to try and secure support for such a move from each of the thirteen colonies. But it was not the consensus opinion among the country's populace, nor even initially of the delegates to the Second Continental Congress, who spent over a year "piddling, twiddling and resolving" as the opening song of the musical "*1776*" described their deliberations.

Lincoln sought to contain the debate about the nation's civic ethos to the cause of preserving the union in the initial years of his presidency in order to avoid having the differing opinions over slavery between the "Unionist" and "Abolitionist" wings of his party split it apart. The scope of the Emancipation Proclamation of 1863 was carefully limited to those slaves in states that were in a state of rebellion against the union in an implicit acknowledgment of the shaky constitutional and political ground his action rested upon.

And while the first one hundred days of Franklin Delano Roosevelt's first term are famous for the plethora of new laws and initiatives they produced that were designed to assert a more central role for the federal government in the country's economic life, most of them were struck down by a Supreme Court whose majority opinions reflected the previous civic ethos of a laissez faire approach to the government's role in the economy.

Each of the three previous periods that followed a major catalytic event were also filled with fear, uncertainty, and doubt about the right way to deal with the radical change in the country's circumstances, which in turn fed a highly polarized and divisive political debate that took years to resolve. The predictability of the nation's reaction to catalytic events was confirmed by the vitriol of the political debate after Obama's seemingly decisive election victory in 2008. Whether it was about stimulus spending or the bank and auto company bailouts, the Affordable Care Act or ObamaCare, or the debt ceiling negotiations, each of the debates followed a predictable path of partisan passion across increasingly hostile political aisles.

The differences of opinion were even sharp enough to give rise to a new political movement, the Tea Party, organized in opposition to each of these attempts by the Obama administration to find new ways to deal with the aftermath of the financial markets collapse in 2008. With an exquisite sense of historical timing, the nature and tenor of the country's political discourse kept rising from one debate to the next until it reached the same fever pitch that engulfed the nation after the three previous catalytic events. Someone who lived from 1773 until 1776, or from 1860 until 1863, or from 1929 until 1933, and was brought back to life to relive the events from 2008 through 2011 would have immediately recognized the contours and emotions of the debate, if not the specific content.

A New Civic Ethos is the Consequence of a Fourth Turning Election

This generational and historical context is important to keep in mind when assessing the importance of President Obama's reelection in 2012. The Colonists' decisive victory in the battle of Yorktown settled the country's eighteenth century civic ethos debate over the virtue of a democratic form of government independent from all royal dictates. Lincoln's re-election in 1864, the passage of the 13th amendment as brilliantly portrayed in the movie "*Lincoln*," and the Confederate surrender at Appomattox shortly thereafter, were rapid fire events that represented the climax of the nation's most bitter civic ethos debate. The outcome made it clear where the majority stood on these nineteenth century questions of both the sanctity of the union and the inability of a country to exist half free and half slave. Franklin Delano Roosevelt's landslide re-election in 1936 was also the climactic event in the debate over the New Deal. Its obvious popularity forced the Supreme Court in 1937 to finally acknowledge the New Deal's constitutional legitimacy as the civic ethos for the United States in the twentieth century.

A review of this history of changes in America's civic ethos due to generational change, makes it clear that President Obama's decisive re-election in 2012, after a bitter year of campaigning on the question of what role the federal government should play in the life of the nation in the twenty-first century, is of the same climactic, decisive nature as these previous historical events. After the election results were in, Republican pollster, Frank Luntz pointed to the historical parallels between President Obama's and Franklin Delano Roosevelt's re-election: "Forty percent of America is ecstatic, 20 percent is accepting and 40 percent thinks the country is going to hell. The only other time we've seen this was FDR in 1936."

As Rick Stengel, the editor of *Time*, wrote in explaining why his magazine named the President its Person of the Year, he (Obama) had "stitched together a winning coalition and perhaps a governing one as well. His presidency spells the end of the Reagan realignment that had defined American politics for 30 years. We are in the midst of historic cultural and demographic changes, and Obama is both the symbol and in some ways the architect of this new America."

Having consciously campaigned on a promise to create a country where "everyone gets a fair shot and everyone does their fair share" rather than the "you're on your own" vision of his opponent, President Obama enters a second term with the opportunity to make his vision the civic ethos of the country for the next forty years. However, to solidify his perspective on what the role of government should be in the twenty-first century, he will need to ensure the continuity and cohesion of the coalition his particular brand of politics has brought to the Democratic Party, even as Republicans seek to find a new basis upon which to build an alternative majority coalition.

CHAPTER THREE:
REMAKING THE GRAND OLD PARTY

The Democratic and Republican parties operate in a nation that is being sharply transformed demographically with its citizens rapidly shifting their lifestyles and beliefs as a result. Because the two parties function within the same environment, each of them must respond to these changes to remain competitive, even as they seek to maintain the support of their traditional constituencies. However, as the outcome of the 2012 election demonstrates, the two parties are in vastly different places in this crucial undertaking.

The Democratic Party needs to solidify and maintain the majority coalition with which it won in 2008 and 2012 and which, because it mirrors the changing American population, offers the prospect of continued electoral success in the years ahead. This is by no means certain or easy, but it is a task of a different magnitude than the one confronting the Republican Party. For the GOP, the job is to develop a new coalition, based on today's and tomorrow's demographics, rather than yesterday's, that will permit it to compete in elections across the nation.

In our first book, *Millennial Makeover*, we described the "Four M's" of politics—money, messenger, media, and message. When the four elements work in synergy and reinforce each other, campaigns and political parties win elections. They, thus, provide a useful framework for analyzing the current competitive positions of the two parties and the path each must follow to be successful and participate effectively in the nation's governance.

It Wasn't All About the Man and His Money

Despite the fears of many Democrats after the Citizens United v. FEC Supreme Court decision eliminating restrictions on corporate contributions that had been part of the United States election law for a century, the first "M"--money--turned out not to be a problem for either major party presidential campaign or national political party in 2012. Although, as in 2008, the Obama campaign was more focused on relatively small contributions than its Republican opponent, both the president's campaign and that of Mitt Romney raised and spent more than $1 billion each. Newly formed super PAC's such as Americans for Prosperity (David and Charles Koch), American Crossroads (Karl Rove), Restore our Future (Mitt Romney) and Priorities USA Action (Barack Obama) took advantage of the Supreme Court decision and, along with the two parties, collected and expended billions more. All told, political expenditures exceeded $6 billion in 2012.

Since both presidential candidates and parties were at relative financial parity, and had enough money to campaign effectively, the other three political "M's" assumed even greater importance in 2012. After a caustic and divisive primary campaign, the GOP chose the one candidate in their field of challengers, Mitt Romney, who seemed to be well positioned to be an effective messenger to carry the battle to President Obama.

Classically handsome, a devoted husband, father, and grandfather with a large, attractive family, Romney looked like someone central casting would choose to be the GOP standard bearer. He also had the right private sector resume for the part, having successfully rescued and run the 2002 Salt Lake City Winter Olympics. His effective, if controversial, operation of a private equity investment firm, Bain Capital, gave credibility to his claim that he "knows what it takes to manage the economy and create jobs."

However, when it came to his political past, Romney played down, if not fully disowned, his moderate record as Governor of Massachusetts. In order to secure the presidential nomination of a party whose ideology was significantly to the right of what his own had previously been, he described himself as "severely conservative," a supporter of right to life legislation, and opposed to tax increases to reduce the federal budget deficit. During the Republican candidate debates, he deliberately took the most extreme position on immigration of the GOP field, suggesting that those here without proper documentation should "self-deport." He also avoided mentioning the program of universal health care coverage that was adopted during his tenure as Governor, and when forced to cite differences between it and "ObamaCare," only said that his program was a state plan while the president's was federal.

After winning the Republican presidential nomination, Romney attempted to tack back to the political center for the fall campaign against President Obama. In a rare moment of candor, Romney advisor, Eric Fehrnstrom, said that in the general election, "It's almost like an Etch-a-Sketch. You can kind of shake it up and restart all over again." But, in real life, such behavior doesn't help a messenger earn the trust of the electorate that person is trying to win over.

As it turned out, the perception that he was a flip-flopper was the least of Romney's problems as the GOP's messenger. During the primaries, he developed an image that he was a plutocrat, almost a personal caricature of the stereotypical Republican, who could not relate to, and cared little about, the worries of middle class Americans. This impression was reinforced by his offer to bet Texas Governor Rick Perry $10,000 to settle a debate disagreement on healthcare policy. Other opponents, such as Newt Gingrich and Rick Santorum, effectively questioned his unwillingness to release more than two years of federal income tax returns, contributing to an impression that his use of exotic tax shelters and obscure sections of the tax code were designed to avoid taxes in ways that the average American could not.

All of these problems with Romney as a messenger were crystallized by the candidate's own words in a video recorded surreptitiously by a bartender at a fundraiser for wealthy donors in Florida. Attempting to explain why he was having so much trouble defeating a "socialist" presiding over a weak economy, Romney suggested the problem wasn't his, but rather the greediness and laziness of a large slice of the American electorate. "There are 47 percent of the people who will vote for the president no matter what, who are dependent upon government, who believe that government has a responsibility to care for them, who believe they are entitled to health care, to food, to housing, to you name it. That's an entitlement and the government should give it to them...These are people who pay no income tax. Forty-seven percent of Americans pay no income tax. So our message of low taxes does not connect...And, my job is not to worry about those people. I'll never convince them that they should take personal responsibility and care for their lives."

Together, these actions and inactions by Romney and his campaign produced an image that Romney was an elitist who would say and do anything to get elected. A Pew survey taken about 10 days before the November election revealed the extent to which these beliefs about Romney had taken hold within the electorate. Voters perceived that Obama rather than Romney took consistent positions on issues (51% to 36%) and connected well with ordinary Americans (59% to 31%). A majority agreed rather than disagreed that "it's hard to know what Romney really stands for" (53% to 44%). These negative perceptions overwhelmed Romney's more narrow advantage over Obama for being better able to improve the job situation (50% to 42%).

Demonstrating the accuracy of John F. Kennedy's aphorism that "victory has a thousand fathers, but defeat is an orphan," Republicans turned on their messenger in droves immediately after his loss. The Republican right attributed Romney's defeat to what it perceived as his failure to be sufficiently conservative. Typical was this comment by Jenny Beth Martin of the Tea Party Patriots: "We wanted someone who would fight for us. What we got was a weak, moderate candidate hand-picked by the Beltway elites and country club establishment wing of the Republican Party."

From the perspective of some Republican governors, such as Louisiana's Bobby Jindal, (an Indian-American) and New Mexico's Susana Martinez (a Mexican-American), the problem was Romney's unwillingness or inability to reach out beyond his party's white male base. Romney didn't improve his image with the public by saying in his first post-election TV interview that President Obama had won reelection through "targeted gifts" to minorities and Millennials such as healthcare "in perpetuity," "amnesty" to the children of illegal immigrants, forgiveness of college loan debts, and free contraception coverage through ObamaCare.

There is no denying that Mitt Romney was a flawed candidate, with many of his wounds being self-inflicted. However, there is also no evidence that any of the others who contested Romney for the GOP nomination would have fared any better against Obama than Romney did. Rick Santorum, who was the last Romney primary opponent left standing, was the grandson of an Italian immigrant coal miner, who had the potential to appeal to blue collar voters, unlike Romney who had grown up as the son of an automotive CEO in an upper class environment. But Santorum's positions on virtually all issues were generally more conservative than those espoused by Romney, making it unlikely that he would have won the votes of many of the Millennials, minorities, and women who are the core of the Obama Democratic coalition and of America's electorate in the 21st century in a general election.

In the end, focusing on the remaining two political "M's"—media and message—rather than casting all, or even most, of the blame for the GOP's difficulties on the party's most recent messenger, Mitt Romney, provides a clearer picture of what happened in 2012 and what the Republican Party must do to compete effectively in the future.

The Media Are Not the Message

In *Millennial Makeover* we pointed out that one of the factors underpinning the political realignments that occur about every four decades in the United State is a change in mass communication technology or media that creates a different way to communicate with and persuade greater numbers of voters more effectively. From the telegraph and rotary press in the 19th century to radio and television in the 20th, new communication technologies have been an important factor in the massive changes that have periodically transformed American politics.

In the 21st century, strikingly new communication technologies—the Internet and Internet-based social networking—have transformed the nature of political campaigns. Unlike the broadcast media that dominated political campaigns in the 20th century, however, the Internet permits anyone and everyone to immediately share, on a regular basis, news, information, and political events with individuals they actually know. By 2012, almost half (47%) of American voters used the Internet as a source for news about the campaign, far surpassing newspapers, radio and magazines, and rivaling the use of television (67%). As a result, just as was the case with the telegraph, radio, and television before them, politicians have increasingly turned to the Internet and social networking to get their message across. Howard Dean was the first to use the Internet extensively in his run for the Democratic presidential nomination in 2004. But it was the presidential campaigns of Barack Obama, in 2008 and again in 2012, that fully embraced the power of the Internet and social networking and placed its usage at the center of the campaign's strategy. The Obama campaign created highly interactive web sites designed not simply to communicate with, but ultimately to mobilize, its potential supporters. Its primary goal was to translate online interactivity to offline action—volunteering, word-of-mouth persuasion, financial contributions and voting.

Starting with the Iowa caucuses in January 2008, the Obama campaign effectively used the Internet to mobilize previously low turnout groups—Millennials and minorities—to upend Hillary Clinton's Democratic presidential nomination run. The Obama campaign's use of the Internet both as a voter mobilization and fundraising tool was equally effective in the fall against John McCain. An analysis by a Lansing, Michigan Internet consulting firm, the Spartan Internet Political Performance Index (SIPP), calculated the overall Internet usage share of each presidential candidate, indicating that by the time Obama clinched the Democratic nomination in 2008 his Internet share was about twice that of Clinton. By the time he was elected president in November Obama's SIPP share was about 65 to McCain's 35.

Obama's clear edge in using the new technology continued in his reelection victory over Mitt Romney. In fact, the president's SIPP share advantage over Romney (70 to 30) was even greater than it had been over McCain. An October 2012 Google survey of 2,500 Internet users indicated that 64 percent believed that the president's campaign was more adept at social media and online persuasion than the Romney campaign. A Pew analysis during the general election campaign suggests a number of reasons for this perception.

First, the Obama campaign was far more active online than Romney's. The president's reelection organization posted nearly four times more content on almost twice as many platforms and engendered twice as many responses from users. Obama's Internet effort was not simply better in quantity, but also in quality. In 2012, the Obama campaign added state-by-state content pages containing local information that site visitors could use in their own communities.

As in 2008, Obama's online activities targeted a far greater number of specific voter groups than his GOP opponent (18 to 9). Unlike 2008, when it posted press clips about the candidate and campaign, its website no longer contained a "news" section with media stories. In 2012, according to Pew, "the only news of the day comes directly from the Obama campaign itself." All of this permitted the campaign to better control the information reaching its potential supporters.

An article by technology writer, Sean Gallagher, with the apt title, "How Team Obama's Tech Efficiency Left Romney IT in [the] Dust," points to what may have been the best explanation for the Obama campaign's Internet advantage: the Obama effort was internal to the campaign, rather than "outsourced" to consultants as was the Romney campaign's, leading to greater efficiency and flexibility: "The Obama campaign spent a seventh of what the Romney campaign spent on digital and an even smaller fraction of what Romney spent on voter and donor contact...In the end, the deciding factor wasn't what the Obama campaign spent money on, but what it did with all that money. Insourcing gave the campaign a strategic flexibility that the Romney campaign lacked...And reduced reliance on outside consultants allowed the Obama campaign to direct capital toward places where it had a bigger impact—such as advertising, where the Obama campaign outspent Romney by a factor of 5 to 1."

It's Not Your Grandfather's Electorate Anymore

The Romney campaign also suffered in comparison with President Obama's in its attempts to gather reliable information about the electorate. As the *New Republic's* Noam Scheiber put it, the Romney campaign perceived the electorate from a "best-case" rather than "worst-case" perspective. It assumed that most everything of importance occurring in the campaign, including the composition of the voting population would break Romney's way. Romney's campaign polling expected the electorate to look as it did a decade or two ago not as it looks now, perhaps the most egregious error of a very flawed campaign.

Specifically, the Romney campaign assumed that key components of Obama's Democratic coalition—Millennials and minorities—would not turn out at the rate that they did in 2008, leaving the electorate about as heavily white and elderly as it had been in earlier presidential contests. In fact, however, Millennial and minority turnout was at the level it was in 2008 or even higher. This stemmed in part from the Obama campaign's strong turnout efforts, but also because Millennials and minorities made up a larger portion of the population in 2012 than they had four years earlier, let alone the more distant past.

In addition, the Romney campaign assumed an "enthusiasm gap" that separated the supporters of each candidate. Romney supporters were believed to be more interested in the election and, therefore, likely to turn out at a substantially higher rate than Obama's. In Pew's final pre-election survey Romney voters did seem more engaged than Obama's on most political commitment measures—thinking about the election, following the campaign, and stated likelihood of voting. However, Obama voters were more likely than Romney's to strongly support their candidate (81% to 73%), suggesting that the degree of commitment to a candidate may be a better indicator of turnout probability than more abstract and less direct measures of campaign interest.

Finally, according to Scheiber, the Romney team believed that, in a closely divided electorate, it would be independents, rather than those who identify with one of the parties, that would determine the outcome of the election. Romney's polling indicated that, in most of the crucial battleground states, the independents were breaking toward the GOP candidate. Pew's final national survey confirmed that Romney led Obama among independents 44 percent to 41 percent with 15 percent still undecided. The problem for Romney, however, was that the electorate wasn't as closely divided as it had been just a few years earlier. Instead, since 2004, the balance between Democratic and Republican identifiers within the American electorate had widened to the advantage of the Democratic Party.

In 2000, the Democrats had a narrow party ID advantage among likely voters of two percentage points (35% to 33%). In 2004, when the Republicans had a party ID lead of two percentage points over the Democrats (37% to 35%), the partisan balance was even better for the GOP. By contrast, in 2008, the Democrats had a six percentage party ID lead over the GOP among likely voters (37% to 31%). And, in 2012, when Obama achieved a four point popular vote win over Mitt Romney, the Democrats had a four point party ID advantage among Pew's likely voters (36% to 32%). The changing demographics of the American electorate undoubtedly had something to do with this, as did a worsening perception of the GOP. Regardless of the reason, the Democratic Party started with a wider than previous party identification advantage, lessening the importance of the independent voter in determining election results.

Big Data Beats Big Money

If the Romney campaign's polling was questionable, the results of its voter identification and get-out-the-vote programs were disastrous. These programs were called ORCA, a dig at Obama's Narwhal program. (In the Arctic, the Orca killer whale is a natural predator of the smaller Narwhal whale). While the ultimate goal of these two programs was to maximize the turnout of their candidate's voters in crucial battleground states, each went about this in a different way.

ORCA was designed to predict the election's outcome. If Romney's vote met specific turnout targets within each key state, his campaign could project a Romney win in that state. This capability was merely a side benefit of the program created by the Obama campaign. Instead, Narwhal and a related voter ID program, Dream Catcher, were designed to gather and integrate data about individual voters from a variety of sources. These programs allowed the Obama campaign to target voters by demographics, issue concerns, vote intention, likelihood of turnout, and psychographics such as hopes and dreams, fears and frustrations.

According to Jason Bloomberg, of Zap Think, the possible benefits of ORCA were hindered by the Romney campaign's reliance on best-case scenarios: "Fundamentally, the Republicans used their tool with an expectation of victory. So ORCA gave them evidence of that victory—disastrously misleading evidence...In contrast the Democrats used their tool with no expectations of the result. They allowed Narwhal to inform them about the nuggets of useful information it gleaned from the raw data, enabling the Obama team to take actions that would eventually lead to success, even if they wouldn't have guessed such actions would have been efficacious without such information." But ORCA's difficulties went beyond the outcomes expected by its users. The program suffered from major operational flaws that became evident on Election Day. First, ORCA was developed in only seven months, after Romney clinched the Republican presidential nomination. As a result, once the program was developed, it was never fully pretested under live conditions. Moreover, ORCA's ultimate users—Romney volunteers in the battleground states—were never given meaningful hands-on training in the use of the program. The information packets given volunteers did not reach them until the night before Election Day and required volunteers to print 60-page PDF instructions even to see those instructions in an easily readable format. Many Romney volunteers were also not given valid credentials that would allow them access to the polling places to which they had been assigned or valid passwords that would permit them to access ORCA online. Finally, on Election Day, the untested ORCA program crashed for several hours due to bandwidth constraints and Internet servers that shut down under real life conditions, thinking they were under attack from hackers.

The Obama campaign's use of Narwhal was far different. Obama had the advantage of running for reelection four years after his team developed a widely heralded voter ID and online effort. In the expectation that the president would run again in 2012, his team did not dismantle their programs after the 2008 campaign, but neither did it rest on its laurels. In fact, Narwhal and Dream Catcher were designed to patch flaws in the campaign's IT programs: "During the first initial steps of the campaign in 2007, each Obama campaign department started creating their own data repositories for the election and voter data they collected. They realized, albeit too late for the 2008 elections, that they were collecting unprecedented volumes of political information, but had no way to study the data together to yield the maximum benefit...Even as the outside world marveled at their technical prowess, Obama campaign staffers were exasperated at what seemed like a basic system failure: They had records on 170 million voters, 13 million online supporters, three million campaign donors and at least as many volunteers—but no way of knowing who among them were the same people." The data integration capabilities of Narwhal were designed to fix that flaw.

The Obama campaign's computer based micro-targeting also allowed it to make more efficient and effective use of traditional media than Romney's. Marcus Stern and Tim McLaughlin pointed out that "The Obama team used the fragmentation of cable TV's audience to its fullest advantage to target tailored messages to voters in battleground states. Meanwhile, Romney's campaign relied on a more traditional mass saturation of broadcast TV. The Romney campaign was entirely dark on cable TV for two of the campaign's last seven days."

Moreover, Obama often spent far less than Romney for ads aired by the same stations during the same shows. In part, this was because Obama could reserve ad spots at lower rates in the winter and spring of 2012 while Romney was still trying to win the Republican nomination. But, it also could be attributed to the decisions of the one harried and overworked person at The Stevens and Schriefer Group to which the campaign outsourced its entire media buy. By contrast, the Obama campaign internally had thirty full-time media buyers to plan, negotiate, and place its TV ads. In addition, many of the Romney campaign's TV ads were bought and paid for by the newly formed SuperPacs, which were not eligible for the lower rates that must be offered to political campaigns under the FEC's rules.

If Media's Not the Answer, What Is?

In the aftermath of its 2012 loss it didn't take long for the Republican Party to acknowledge its deficit across virtually all facets of contemporary political media. In March 2013, Republican

National Committee Chairman, Reince Priebus, announced a detailed plan to rebuild the GOP, focused primarily on rebranding, campaign mechanics, technology, and the nominating process.

From the 1970s into the 1990s, the Democratic Party faced the same problems as the GOP does today and tried many of the same solutions to those problems that Priebus' "Growth and Opportunity" report recommends. For example, back then a series of commissions charted by the national Democratic Party, including one chaired by one of the co-authors of this book (Morley Winograd), changed the party's rules so that the Democratic National Convention was more likely to nominate presidential candidates with broader appeal to the electorate than George McGovern had demonstrated in 1972. The futility of such efforts was clearly revealed in the repeated nomination of presidential candidates throughout the 1980s who were soundly defeated by their Republican opponents. The lesson was learned again in 2008 when Barack Obama's campaign used its organizing skills to secure the delegates he needed for his nomination disproportionately in states that chose delegates in caucuses rather than primaries, a method that prior Democratic Party rules commissions had tried to limit.

In the end, fixes like those tried by the Democrats three or four decades ago and recommended by Reince Priebus in 2013 are at best, a necessary, but not sufficient, condition of enhancing the GOP's prospects in future presidential elections. Just as its messenger was not the Republican's biggest problem in 2012, neither ultimately was its use of political media or the way it ran campaigns. As Justin Fox, the Editorial Director of the *Harvard Business Review*, pointed out in a perceptive article, published soon after Priebus announced his party rebuilding proposals, "the GOP needs a new product" (or message) to appeal to the emerging electorate that will shape American politics in the 21st century, not simply more effective use of political media.

However, although Reince Priebus spoke of a need to change just about everything in the way the Republican Party operates, nominates candidates, and conducts campaigns he explicitly rejected the necessity of a change in the party's message: "To be clear, our principles are sound. Our principles are not old rusty thoughts in some book. Freedom and opportunity are ever-fresh, revolutionary ideas. They are the road-map for American renewal in a new and interconnected world. *But...the way we communicate our principles isn't resonating widely enough."*

Many Democratic activists can still recall the Reverend Jesse Jackson saying almost exactly the same thing about how the Democratic Party could reclaim the presidency after the 1988 defeat of a different Massachusetts Governor, Michael Dukakis. The notion that changing only three of the four M's of politics, but not the message, would be enough to bring victory turned out not to be true back then and it remains just as untrue today.

Perhaps because of how much the Democratic Party eventually changed its message in the 1990s, many conservative Republicans, seemed overly anxious to nip the relatively innocuous Priebus recommendations in the bud. Tea Party leader, Jenny Beth Martin, condemned the report and its recommendations, "Americans and those in the Tea Party movement don't need an autopsy report from the RNC to know the Republicans failed to promote our principles and lost because of it."

Rush Limbaugh also vigorously attacked the effort, proclaiming what he thought the GOP's problem to be: "The Republicans are just totally bamboozled right now... they're entirely lacking in confidence...The Republican Party lost because it's not conservative." In an imaginary discussion with Priebus, Limbaugh cited and rejected one of the concerns raised by the RNC report: "Our party's [perceived to be] narrow-minded...So we gotta be more tolerant. That means we cash in our chips on our core principles," something Limbaugh was clearly not willing to do.

A survey of its readers by *Conservative HQ*, which bills itself as "the online news source for conservatives and Tea Partiers," indicated that 95 percent "agreed with Rush [that] if the GOP moves away from championing values, such as traditional marriage, it will lose support." Only 3 percent "agreed with Priebus, the GOP must change and broaden its appeal by abandoning traditional values." At its first meeting after the release of the report, held in Hollywood to demonstrate how much the party was committed to change, members of the Republican National Committee also agreed with

Rush and overwhelmingly passed a resolution defending traditional marriage. Clearly, many on the GOP right do not want to go where they believe their leader, despite his protestations to the contrary, wants to lead them.

Even many Millennial Republicans, while saying that their party is out of step on issues like gay marriage and immigration reform, believe that the GOP's path to renewal is one based solely on rebranding and better use of new technology, something their generation is well-positioned to provide. In a BuzzFeed article about those tech-savvy young Republicans, Zeke Miller said "younger Republicans...almost universally rejected the notion that the party has gone broadly astray—it just has a communications problem." Miller quoted College Republican National Committee chairman Alex Schriver: "Everyone agrees we have some demographic concerns, but we didn't lose on principles or ideas. Our packaging lost, and we have to improve the way we communicate our message to young and Hispanic voters."

The Message is (Almost) Everything

For the Republican Party, however, message is a problem; in fact, it is the GOP's core problem as it attempts to regain its footing in 21st century America. As the Washington Post's,Chris Cillizza and Sean Sullivan wrote right after Reince Priebus announced his program of party reform, "...there is the larger (and more important) question of whether fixing the mechanics of the party—outreach to minorities, data mining, etc.—can fix the message of the party." That message impedes the way in which the GOP is perceived by the emerging demographics that are both the core of Barack Obama's majority Democratic voting coalition and America's 21st century electorate.

Similarly, Matthew Cooper, writing in the National Journal,argued that structural reforms alone wouldn't be enough to revive the fortunes of the GOP. Citing the research of political scientist Samuel Popkin, Cooper wrote that "for all the money spent in campaigns on information and disinformation, polls and ads, most voters basically know what they're getting in the two candidates and make a rational decision. They aren't deceived. They have absorbed the philosophies of the candidates, know their positions on the most important issues...If parties win because of ideas, then the Priebus plan, with its quotidian emphasis on process...won't work...Ideas are going to make the GOP competitive in presidential elections."

What's a Party to Do?

At this point, however, it appears that few within the Republican Party seem willing to take on the task of reshaping the party's message to bring it into closer accord with the beliefs of the nation's emerging electorate, instead preferring to focus on less controversial and perhaps easier to achieve structural and technological reforms. Historically, these types of ideological differences ultimately are resolved within a political party in the course of its presidential nominating campaigns. Republican consultant, Mike Murphy, sees this as a likely outcome. "We'll be stuck in an age of chaos and factional warlords for a while. The battle royal will be the 2016 presidential primary season."

The question, however, is whether significant ideological differences still exist among the various factions in the Republican Party—religious conservatives, Tea Partiers, the business establishment, and hardcore libertarians—and therefore how much inclination there will be to take on such a fight in whatever venue it might occur. Pew survey researcher, Andrew Kohut, indicates that factional differences within the Republican Party are not as great as some believe. "For decades, my colleagues and I have examined the competing forces and coalitions within the two parties. In our most recent assessments, we found not only that the percentage of people self-identifying as Republicans has hit historic lows, but that within that smaller base, the traditional divides between pro-business economic conservatives and social conservatives had narrowed. There was less diversity of values within the GOP than at any time in the past quarter-century."

About four decades ago the Democratic Party was in straits very similar to those of the GOP today. The Democratic New Deal coalition that had dominated U.S. electoral politics and shaped public policy fell apart under the strain of generational and racial change. From the late 1960s into the 1990s, the Democratic Party's message and imagery were as out of sync with the America of that era as the Republicans' are today. As Kohut pointed out, "In my decades of polling, I recall only one moment when a party had been driven as far from the center as the Republican Party has been today. The outsize influence of hard line elements in the party is doing to the GOP what supporters of Gene McCarthy and George McGovern did to the Democratic Party—radicalizing its image and standing in the way of its revitalization."

Democratic Party history also provides the best model for the GOP to imitate to regain its competitive edge. The Democratic Leadership Council (DLC), founded by a former Senate staffer, Al From, in 1985 after Ronald Reagan's drubbing of Walter Mondale, developed the ideas that allowed the Democratic Party to finally begin to compete effectively in the more conservative political era of the late 20th century.

From believed strongly that "ideas matter." The DLC's overarching position was that in the America of the late 20th century, economic populism and doctrinaire liberalism were not as viable as they had been in the earlier New Deal era. The organization's philosophy, instead, was built on "progressive ideals, mainstream values, and innovative, non-bureaucratic, market-based solutions." His organization created an alternative brand, New Democrats, built on the values of "opportunity, responsibility and community."

The chairman of the DLC, Governor Bill Clinton, took that message around the country, organizing groups of like-minded Democrats to come to an alternative convention in 1991 that offered a "new choice" in American politics. As described in the book, *Taking Control*, the DLC gained more prominence than might have been expected by purposefully contrasting its program with those of its liberal detractors, particularly Jesse Jackson. Although initially it had little hope of wresting the 1992 presidential nomination from the more mainstream liberal Democrats of that era, the DLC's marketing plan was based upon finding a candidate who could use the matching funds for presidential primary campaigns to finance the publicizing of its ideas across the country. The plan succeeded beyond the wildest imagination of its authors with the nomination and election of Bill Clinton, who then governed as a DLC centrist.

Under his leadership, a range of DLC developed and endorsed policies—welfare reform, NAFTA (the North American Free Trade Agreement), charter schools and other parental school choice measures, expanded health insurance through tax credits, and an expansion of the Earned Income Tax Credit—were enacted.

The DLC's message was the right one for Democrats to offer in an era dominated by conservative politics. But by 2011, even Al From recognized the country had changed again, and he dissolved the DLC. Still, in its time, it must be acknowledged that the organization he created successfully rebuilt and redirected the Democratic Party, moving it from the political wilderness to electoral competitiveness and policy prominence. The Republican Party could certainly benefit by considering the DLC's approach as a road-map for its revival in this new era.

That however may take a while. After all, the DLC did not arrive until nearly two decades after the New Deal era of Democratic Party dominance ended in 1968. Nor does any group within the Republican Party currently have the same intellectual and political power that the DLC built within the Democratic Party over a decade. Whenever that nucleus of leaders does emerge and is willing to take on their party's establishment and most committed supporters, the country will know that the Republican Party is once again ready to swim in the political mainstream of 21st century America.

CHAPTER FOUR:
WILL THE DEMOCRATS KEEP ON, KEEPIN' ON?

During the past decade, through a fortuitous combination of strategic thinking and being in the right place at the right time, the Democratic Party has taken advantage of the demographic changes reshaping America to assemble a majority voting coalition that puts the party in position to dominate U.S. elections and shape public policy for the next twenty or thirty years. Maintaining that coalition in the years ahead, however, is no easy task. In fact, it may turn out to be more difficult for the Democrats to preserve their coalition than it was to put it together in the first place.

Justin Fox, in his *Harvard Business Review* article that primarily focused on the Republicans' proposed reforms, raised serious questions about the ultimate stability of the newly created Democratic alignment: "...the current Democratic mix of affluent professionals, minorities, unionized workers and the young isn't exactly a natural coalition." It is debatable whether any political party coalition is "natural," but he is right to point out that Democrats can take nothing for granted. It will require a concerted effort by all the leaders of the Democratic Party, particularly President Obama, for the party to maintain the voter alignment that led to Democratic victories in 2008 and 2012 at the presidential level.

Recent survey research suggests that at the moment, at least, the Democratic Party coalition is solidifying. In a compilation of its 2012 political polls, Pew indicated that the Democrats held a wide lead over the Republicans in party identification among the core components of its coalition: women (52% to 39%), Millennials (55% to 36%), African-Americans (87% to 8%), Hispanics (61% to 29%), college graduates (51% to 43%), Jews (66% to 28%), those unaffiliated with any faith (63% to 26%), and residents of the Northeastern (54% to 37%) and Pacific Coast (53% to 38%) states. This is good news for the Democrats since political science research suggests that, once formed, the party identifications of most individuals remain stable for a lifetime.

To ensure its continued dominance of national politics in the years ahead, the Democratic Party will have to pay just as much attention to the "Four M's" of politics as Republicans will.

Spreading the Mother's Milk of Politics Around

If money is the mother's milk of politics, the Republicans have historically been more productive dairy farmers than the Democrats. Beginning in at least 1896 when Mark Hanna, who headed William McKinley's presidential campaign, raised and spent what was, at the time, the stupendous sum of $3.5 million, seven times the funds and expenditures of the Democratic nominee, William Jennings Bryan, the GOP has almost invariably enjoyed a clear financial edge over the Democratic Party. The Republicans' monetary advantage persisted even during the Democratic-dominated New Deal era. In 1936, a month prior to his landslide reelection victory, Franklin Roosevelt complained that his campaign did not have enough money to pay its headquarters staff. In 1948, a lack of money stranded Harry Truman's whistle stop campaign train in Oklahoma.

Under the presidency of Bill Clinton, however, Democrats began a strong effort to at least achieve financial parity with Republicans. President Clinton's obsession with raising money, which stemmed from the vow he made after losing re-election as Governor of Arkansas to never be outspent by his opponent again, left some scandals in its wake but it also infused his party with the same determination he had to match Republican campaign money, dollar for dollar. When candidate Howard Dean discovered a new source of money in his brief 2004 primary campaign by raising lots of it in small amounts on the Internet, the fortuitous marriage of technology and campaign fund-raising became a staple of all Democratic campaigns thereafter.

While not eschewing large contributions, Obama used the Internet in 2008 to supplement more traditional fundraising efforts. Through October 15 of that year, Obama raised $639 million compared to John McCain's $375 million. About $500 million, or 78 percent, of Obama's total came from three million individual donors who contributed less than $200 each. This fundraising proficiency enabled the Obama campaign to become the first of a major party in more than three decades to reject public financing.

In 2012, the Obama campaign, the Democratic National Committee (DNC) and Priorities USA, the Obama super PAC raised and spent about $1 billion. This matched the collections and expenditures of the Romney campaign, the Republican National Committee, and Restore Our Future, Romney's super PAC. As was the case four years earlier, however, a majority (57%) of Obama's individual contributors gave less than $200. Only 11 percent came from those contributing the legal maximum of $2500. By contrast, only a quarter of Romney's donors gave less than $200 while a plurality (39%) contributed $2500 or more. Although Republican SuperPacs raised more money than their Democratic counterparts in 2012, their efforts were diffuse enough, both in the campaigns they focused upon and in the messages they delivered, that neither Obama nor Congressional Democrats experienced the overwhelming financial disadvantage that they had feared when the Supreme Court's *Citizens United* decision was first announced.

Not surprisingly, other political organizations have followed the Obama campaign online and are using the Internet to reach out constantly to individual contributors across America. In effect, this means that campaigning and fundraising never ends. On the Democratic side, these almost daily solicitations tell lurid tales about how Republican big givers threaten to overwhelm Democratic candidates and ask for small contributions to prevent that from happening. For Republicans, the influence of big labor and the president's fund-raising prowess provide a similar fear factor to encourage their potential givers.

For the moment, anyway, the power of Internet fundraising targeting small contributors has enabled the Democratic Party to compete financially with the Republicans on roughly even terms. As a result, the first political "M"—money—is not likely to be a major barrier to the Democratic Party in solidifying its majority voter coalition. If, in the future, small donor fundraising proves to be difficult for the Democrats, it will signal that the party's problems are far deeper than its finances alone.

Can the Democrats' High-Tech Pitchers Hold the Lead?

No serious observer doubts that, bolstered by its technological supremacy, the Democratic Party now holds a clear lead over the GOP in almost all phases of the second political "M"—media. For example, the Obama campaign was able to use its sophisticated voter database to make about 150 million contacts, including volunteer recruitment and voter turnout messages. By contrast the RNC's centralized voter database logged only about half as many interactions-- 80.5 million voter contacts, including 14.5 million door-knocks in battleground states and another 900,000 in highly competitive races outside of the presidential battleground states.

Taking steps to improve its lagging performance in this area was a major focus of the GOP's "Growth and Opportunity" report, announced by RNC Chairman Reince Priebus, on what the Republican Party needed to do to get back in the game. After it was issued, Priebus announced a major $10 million investment in all aspects of the party's ground game, going so far as to open a field office in heavily Democratic San Francisco for the sole purpose of engaging northern California's high-tech community.

There are those who believe that Republicans will have difficulty attracting the Silicon Valley's top talent no matter how proximate their offices might be. In a post-election article in San Jose's Mercury News, GOP consultant, Kevin Spillane , pointed out that, "Technologists are often single, socially moderate-to-liberal, much more secular than the population as a whole, and those demographics are a problem for the Republican Party right now." Johnvey Hwang, a young software engineer concurred, "It's hard to side with a party that's still trying to reach out to their base of creationists." Confirming these comments, Santa Clara County, California, at the center of the Silicon Valley, gave 70 percent of its votes to Barack Obama in 2012, while 85 percent of the valley's tech employees who donated to a presidential campaign in 2012, gave money to Obama.

Still, it would be no surprise if the Republican Party eventually assembled a corps of knowledgeable and proficient people to move its technological efforts into the 21st century. Not everyone with high-tech savvy and creativity is a Democrat. Some are libertarians who may find at least that aspect of the GOP's ideological leanings appealing. A few may even be more traditional conservatives. And, regardless of their personal political leanings, some simply may be willing to accept challenging and high-paying work with the Republicans.

Moreover, historically, while one party has normally vaulted to the lead in its use of the newest communication technology, the other has invariably caught up and sometimes passed the original leader in the use of that technology. This was certainly true of television.

Initially, the Democrats benefited from the rapid spread of TV in the 1950s. In 1960, it was the cool and crisp performance by the telegenic John Kennedy against the pale, sweaty, and haggard Richard Nixon in the first televised president debate in U.S. history that put Kennedy narrowly ahead for the first time in a closely contested election, a lead he never relinquished. Four years later, Barry Goldwater's strident acceptance speech and the harsh treatment of New York Governor Nelson Rockefeller at the Republican convention by Goldwater's conservative followers, both of which were televised to the nation, probably cost Goldwater whatever slim chance he may have had to upset Lyndon Johnson.

But, Nixon was a shrewd student of politics. He may have been burned by television in the 1960 election, but he made sure that he would benefit from it in subsequent campaigns. In 1968, he became the first presidential candidate to bring his TV team into the campaign's strategy planning and decision-making. The team did such good work, that one of his critics, Joe McGinnis, complained after the election that Nixon was marketed and packaged like a box of laundry soap.

The 1968 election ended nearly four decades of Democratic electoral dominance and in the years that followed, the GOP continued to maintain its lead in the use of television for political campaigns from the camera-comfortable Ronald Reagan to the carefully staged appearances of George W. Bush. The only Democrat who approached Republicans in the ability to communicate with voters effectively through the tube was also the only Democrat to win two presidential elections in that era, Bill Clinton. Just as Kennedy did to his opponent in 1960, Clinton devastated incumbent President George H.W. Bush with his ability to relate directly to "real voters" asking questions of the candidates directly during their 1992 televised debate, while President Bush was shown on television looking down at his watch to see when his ordeal would be over.

Democrats are not taking their current lead in high-tech communication technology for granted, even as they explore new ways to maximize the use of social and broadcast media to target individual voters on a more personal level. But no technological advantage lasts forever, no matter how sophisticated the effort. For the Democratic Party to maintain its current majority voter coalition, it will have to be based upon the message it conveys to that coalition and the messenger who delivers that message.

The Democrats' 2016 Messenger Must Excel at Coalition Maintenance

When we wrote *Millennial Makeover* about a year and a half before the 2008 presidential election, we were unwilling to hazard a firm prediction about which individual candidate would be elected America's 44th president. We did say, however that Senator Barack Obama was "best positioned among the candidates to capture the hearts and minds of a new generation" and thereby win the White House. At this earlier date, predicting the party nominees and ultimate winner of the 2016 presidential election is even less certain. Nevertheless, we can specify the first and most important task confronting whoever is nominated as the Democratic Party's next messenger.

Regardless of whether Hillary Clinton, Joe Biden, Andrew Cuomo, Martin O'Malley or someone not yet on the D.C. pundits' radar screens wins the Democratic presidential nomination, that person's first order of business will be to maintain and extend the voting coalition that Barack Obama assembled. After McKinley's realigning 1896 win, Theodore Roosevelt, William Howard Taft,

Warren Harding, Calvin Coolidge, and Herbert Hoover all used McKinley's electoral coalition to extend Republican dominance. When Franklin Roosevelt no longer headed the Democratic ticket, other candidates—Harry Truman, John Kennedy, and Lyndon Johnson—relied on the New Deal coalition to keep the White House in Democratic hands. Even when Richard Nixon left the presidency in disgrace, Ronald Reagan, George H.W. Bush, and George W. Bush used the voter coalition that Nixon built to carry GOP electoral dominance into a new century.

In the midst of each of these eras of electoral dominance by one of the parties, the opposing party occasionally nominated and elected appealing and capable candidates to the presidency—Woodrow Wilson, Dwight Eisenhower, and Bill Clinton. Each of them understood and accommodated the unique political circumstances and civic ethos of the era in which they operated. As a result, each won reelection and had successful presidencies, but, as politically and personally adept as they were, none of them was able to transform the prevailing partisan alignment of their time.

In many ways, the Democrats running to succeed President Obama in 2016 will be perceived as seeking a third term for the programs and policies of the Obama administration. Tradition and history suggests that it is a very difficult task to accomplish. Coalitions fall apart over policy differences and personalities over time and it will take all the political skills of the Democratic nominee to preserve the party's electoral unity in the next presidential election. Still, the majority coalition the Democrats have assembled is remarkably unified today, a cohesion built largely upon a solid consensus on what its governing agenda should be. It is therefore likely that whoever is successful in conveying the right message to the Millennial majority coalition that Obama assembled will be the messenger for the party in 2016.

A Democratic Message for the Millennial Era

During the past decade the Democratic Party has assembled a majority voter coalition that reflects the demographics of the 21st century. To maintain that coalition, Democrats must have a message that looks forward to this century and not backward to the demographics and political arguments of the last. So far, the Democrats' message appears to be connecting with the major components of its emerging coalition . On issues ranging from government economic activism and social welfare to foreign policy and from gun control to gay marriage as well as immigration and its impact on the country the components of the Democratic coalition—Millennials, minorities, women, and residents of the Northeast and West—are arrayed against those of the Republican coalition—seniors, whites, men, and those who live in the South.

Ron Brownstein, the most astute and data-savvy of all the Washington reporters, clearly recognizes the emergence and importance of this new Democratic coalition. In a *National Journal* article published two days after Barack Obama's reelection Brownstein wrote, "Loudly, unmistakably, and irreversibly, the Next America announced its electoral arrival this week—years ahead of schedule. The election will likely be remembered not only as a political but also a cultural and social milestone in which the United States suddenly (and for many people, shockingly) realized it was a very different place than it once was. From every direction, social and demographic change was the big story of the results. The key to President Obama's solid Electoral College victory was his advantage among the growing population of non-white voters....Down another track, the massive millennial generation continued to enlarge its influence on American politics."

There are some in Washington, even a few Democrats, who have a very different point of view. Perhaps because they made their political reputations in the last century and have failed to recognize the impact that demographic change has had on Democratic electoral strategies, former Democratic presidential pollsters, and now Fox News commentators, Pat Caddell (Jimmy Carter) and Doug Schoen (Bill Clinton), call for Barack Obama and Democrats to proceed more cautiously on their political agenda. In 2011, at what was admittedly a low point in Obama's first term, Caddell and Schoen even went so far as to suggest Obama step aside as the Democratic Party's 2012 nominee in favor of Hillary Clinton. A year later, after Obama had failed to heed their advice, Caddell and Schoen decided that if they could not have a real Clinton, then perhaps they could persuade the president to at least act like a Clinton. During the 2012 guarantee food and shelter to those needing it. On a key issue that sharply divides the parties, a plurality of Millennials (44%) favor the expansion of ObamaCare, while the greatest number of Boomers (44%) and Silents (46%) want it repealed outright. Millennials also strikingly differ from older generations on dealing with the deficit. A majority of Millennials (55%) favor continued spending to help the economy recover, while majorities of Boomers (51%) and Silents (52%) prefer a stronger focus on deficit reduction. Although they are as likely as older generations to believe that Social Security (81%) and Medicare (87%), the cornerstone policies of New Deal era Democratic activism, have been "good for the country," Millennials do not necessarily prefer that governmental activism take the form of centralized bureaucratic solutions to the nation's problems. But a Democratic message that focuses on federal intervention that supports and encourages local and individual action is likely to be more appealing to Millennials and the other components of the 21st century Democratic coalition than the laissez faire approach now advocated by most Republicans.

· *Foreign policy multilateralism.* Befitting both their orientation toward the welfare of the group and their diversity, Millennials overwhelmingly favor multilateralism rather than the unilateral direction that characterized much of the George W. Bush era foreign policy and that is still advocated by many Republicans. According to Pew, by more than a 2:1 ratio Millennials favor a U.S. foreign policy that takes the interests of our allies into account even if this requires American compromises as opposed to one in which America follows its own self-interest, even if our allies strongly disagree (63% to 29%). A much smaller number of Boomers (49%) prefers a multilateral approach, while a plurality of Silents (44%) favors a unilateral American foreign policy. In addition, a far greater percentage of Millennials (66%), than Boomers (52%) and Silents (49%) believe that "good diplomacy" rather than "military strength" is the best way to ensure peace.

· *Social issues tolerance.* A clear majority of Millennials (68%) in contrast to under half of Boomers (34%) and Silents (38%) favors allowing gays and lesbians to marry one another legally. Similarly a majority of Millennials (65%) support the legalization of marijuana; only 50 percent of Boomers and 32 percent of Silents agree. Indeed, to most Millennials these social issues are holdovers from an earlier era and should be at long last put to rest.

· *Immigration reform and a pathway to citizenship for undocumented immigrants.* Given the sense among Millennials that immigration has benefited America and the fact that one out of every five Millennials has an immigrant parent, it is not surprising that an overwhelming majority of the generation (81%) supports reforming U.S. immigration laws to provide a pathway to citizenship for undocumented immigrants. On this issue, Millennials are joined by solid majorities of Boomers (68%) and Silents (61%), suggesting that this is at least one policy that both political parties could support and enact in some form.

These broad Millennial Generation attitudes give Barack Obama, the next Democratic messenger, and the Democratic Party itself a guidebook to maintaining its majority coalition and possible electoral dominance. Given the electoral change that he and his party have engineered, Barack Obama and the Democratic Party, in spite of lingering misgivings by some Democrats, would seem to have little choice but to design their policy appeals and, hence, their message to fit the needs and wishes of Millennials and the majority coalition they anchor.

This is not the first time that a coalition-forming, and transformational, Democratic president, has been in this situation. In the 1930s, Franklin Roosevelt's "radical" New Deal and, in an echo of the president's critics on Fox News, the "class warfare" that it produced, frightened some conservative Democrats including the party's 1928 presidential nominee, Al Smith, and its former national chairman, John J. Raskob. Both of them endorsed Alf Landon, FDR's 1936 Republican opponent, but Roosevelt persisted in his course anyway and reshaped U.S. politics for the next forty years.

With the right message, Barack Obama and the Democrats have an opportunity to do the same thing eight decades later.

Whether President Obama has the same leadership skills as FDR to enable him to become a transformational president in his own right, however, remains to be determined.

CHAPTER FIVE:
RECONSTRUCTING OBAMA'S PRESIDENTIAL OPPORTUNITY

The person with the most at stake in preserving the new Democratic majority coalition and the one who can do the most to make it a dominant coalition for decades to come is President Barack Obama. His re-election in 2012 gives him the opportunity to be what presidential historian, Stephen Skowronek, calls a "reconstructive" president. There have been five such presidents in American history—Jefferson, Jackson, Lincoln, Franklin D. Roosevelt, and Reagan--each of whom have altered, in Skowronek's words, "the playing field of national politics, durably, substantially, and on his own terms...so that American government itself is understood differently."

To accomplish such an historical task is somewhat a matter of luck, requiring being elected president at the right "political time." But once given the opportunity, a president must also deftly exercise all four P's of presidential leadership—politics, public relations, policy and performance---in ways that alter not just American government but the country's political dynamics as well. The country's current political debates provide evidence that both conditions necessary for a reconstructive presidency--the right timing and the need for skilled execution of the four presidential P's--exist today. Whether Barack Obama will be successful in harnessing this historical opportunity to his own vision remains the single largest unanswered question of the President's second term.

Earning the right to be called a "reconstructive" president by historians is not about how much a president gets done during his time in office but whether during his tenure, "new interests secure a firm grip on power, ...institutional relationships are rearranged to support them, ...governmental priorities are durably recast, and...a corresponding set of legitimating ideas becomes the new common sense" or civic ethos. It is against these four criteria that President Obama's presidency will be judged.

Timing is Important

As Skowronek points out, for these kinds of transformative changes to take place, there must first be what generational theorists call a "catalytic event" that undermines the credibility of the existing regime, throwing it on the defensive. This certainly was the case with the financial collapse of 2008, which revealed the underlying weakness of the Reagan era ideology of deregulation that had significantly reduced government oversight of the economy. The fact that this collapse occurred during the 2008 presidential campaign and that the Republican standard-bearer, John McCain, insisted "that the fundamentals of the American economy are strong," made it much easier for Obama to repudiate the existing set of political assumptions and insist that major change was necessary. One of the reasons President Obama continued to cite this meltdown during the 2012 election, even after he had presided over the economy for four years, was the critical importance that demolishing the credibility of the previous political regime plays in making transformative change possible.

Skowronek points out that "transformative presidencies are forged through an extended series of unsettling political contests [that] usually extend over the course of two full terms." If history is any guide, "the critical tests come after the midterm elections and in reaction to mounting resistance. The test is whether the president will be able to maintain his repudiative authority... [and] deploy it to stigmatize those who continue to resist as extremists and to follow through with more systemic changes." Certainly the rhetoric and actions of President Obama, ever since the failed attempt to reach an agreement with Speaker Boehner on a "grand bargain" to settle the debate over raising the debt ceiling in 2011, would seem to fit this historical pattern.

From that decisive moment on, through his re-election campaign and after it, commentators noticed a new aggressive posture from Obama that sought to repudiate the core of Republican beliefs and stigmatize as extremists those who kowtowed to the

Tea Party's ideology. All of this would suggest the time is ripe for President Obama to emerge as a transformative president by the end of his second term.

There are however, contrary historical precedents that raise questions about whether, in fact, the time is right for a successful reconstructive presidency. Skowronek points out that the two reconstructive presidencies of the twentieth century—Franklin Roosevelt and Ronald Reagan—each came to power after not one, but two, previous assaults on the fundamental political paradigms, or civic ethos, of their day, each more "direct and strident" than the next, had failed.

For example, Woodrow Wilson's progressive critique of the existing civic ethos was more "direct and strident" than Grover Cleveland's, but he was ultimately unsuccessful in making it the "new common sense" in American politics. Wilson would not even have had the chance to try to remake the Democratic Party into the center of progressive thinking if Theodore Roosevelt hadn't bolted the Republican Party in despair over his own party's resistance to this new concept of the role of government in the economy. But Wilson was unable to take advantage of the opportunity presented to him when Roosevelt's Progressive (Bull Moose) Party split the reigning Republican coalition. Under Wilson, America became bogged down in an ultimately unpopular war and pursued a foreign policy that was too interventionist for the times.

It was not until after the GOP returned to power in the 1920's and reasserted its belief that government should take a "hands off" attitude toward the economy, only to see that theory's credibility shattered by the catalytic event of the Great Depression, that the political time was right for Franklin Roosevelt to become a reconstructive president. Even then it took all of FDR's extraordinary political skills to sweep the Republican Party's civic ethos, at least temporarily, into the dustbin of history, and remake the Democratic Party into the home of progressive public policy.

Richard Nixon's attacks on the civic ethos consensus that FDR created were also much more direct than the type of "trimming" that Eisenhower attempted in the 1950's. But nothing in his aborted presidency, or that of Gerald Ford that followed, was remotely as successful in undoing the assumptions of the New Deal as the election of a president, Ronald Reagan, who declared that "government wasn't the solution, it was the problem."

President Carter's presidency represented more of an attempt to re-establish trust in the office of the president than it did an attempt to repudiate President Nixon's policy ideas. Indeed, the first seeds of the fruit of Reagan's deregulation approach were planted during his presidency. Similarly, Bill Clinton didn't bother to try and destroy the dogmas of the Reagan era. He even famously declared in his 1996 State of the Union address that "the era of big government is over." His support of the reinventing government initiative under the direction of Vice President Al Gore was designed to use the ideas of markets and enterprise efficiency to accomplish a different set of more distinctively Democratic goals, but not to undermine the prevailing political consensus that smaller government was better than big government.

It's not at all clear, therefore, that Barack Obama took office at a time when the foundation of the GOP's civic ethos of less taxation, spending, and government regulation had been sufficiently undermined by his recent Democratic predecessors for Obama's even more "direct and strident" attacks on the castle walls of Reagan era verities to be successful.

Devotees of President Obama have some hope for his success, however, because no one can be sure that political time operates at the same historical pace in the 21st Century, impervious to advances in communication technologies, organizational techniques, campaign fund-raising and other changes in the country's political infrastructure. Indeed, the 20th Century experience may have been the exception that proves Skowronek's rule.

The 19th Century's history of reconstructive presidents suggests an entirely different pattern in the pace of change. Jefferson and Jackson, honored today as the founders of the Democratic Party, took first and second successful swings, not third strikes, at returning the federal government to the more limited role they envisioned the Founding Fathers intended. And Lincoln successfully delivered a knockout punch to the prevailing civic ethos of both existing parties of his day on his first try—and as the presidential candidate of a brand new political party to boot. As Skowronek concedes in his latest book, Presidential Leadership in Political time, "History never repeats itself exactly, so a strict, mechanical application of a model of change drawn strictly from the past is likely to miss as much as it picks up."

Furthermore, the intensity of the Tea Party's efforts to ensure that Congressional Republicans remain true to the orthodoxies of the Reagan revolution, as they interpreted them, has provided the very type of opposition that has historically represented the intransigence of a dying regime in its final phase before an assault topples it from power. In these previous scenarios, as with the Great Recession in this sequence, the catastrophic consequences of following the old ideology become so evident to so many that it doesn't require much effort on the part of the opposition to convince the public to change course and look for a new civic ethos. The unyielding opposition of the GOP majority in the House after its victory in the 2010 midterm election and the Republican Party's determination in the Senate to filibuster any meaningful initiative that the President supported may prove, in historical hindsight, to have provided Obama with the same type of foil that earlier reconstructive presidents needed to ensure popular opinion swung irreversibly to their side.

The idea that President Obama was re-elected at the right political time to become a reconstructive president remains a distinct, if somewhat ambiguous, possibility. But contrary to Shakespearian wisdom, ripeness is not all in politics. Even if the historical timing is right, the question remains as to whether or not Obama has the necessary presidential leadership skills to successfully take advantage of his opportunity. Here again the evidence from his first term, his successful re-election campaign, and his political maneuvering afterwards can be read to either encourage or discourage those hoping for such a transformation of American politics.

Destroying the Old Order

Skowronek provides the best description of the tasks a president must undertake to achieve the outcomes of a transformative presidency. The president must move "decisively against institutions and interests upon which the old politics rested. ...Reconstruction... depends on systematically weakening, perhaps even destroying outright, the infrastructure of the old order, on clearing the political and institutional ground upon which something fundamentally new can take hold."

Much of the frustration of the liberal wing of the Democratic Party with Barack Obama stemmed from his unwillingness to engage in such partisan politics even after taking a "shellacking" in the 2010 midterm elections. There was lots of focus on Policy and Performance in the initial years of his presidency, but way too little Democratically-oriented PR and Politics to satisfy the pent up demand for such an approach from the party's most ideologically committed base.

That frustration evaporated when his re-election campaign blasted away at the corporate sensibilities and policy attitudes of his ultimate opponent, Mitt Romney. Taking a stand that some of the more centrist figures in the Democratic Party actually criticized, the President sought to wage a campaign designed, if not to cause class warfare, at least to split the GOP coalition wide open. Using tactics that would have made the GOP's most infamous and successful campaign manager, Lee Atwater, proud, the President first raised a policy idea in the context of his governing authority and then used the GOP's knee jerk reaction against it to ensure the loyalty of the new political interests he needed to attract to build a new majority Democratic coalition. From an endorsement of gay marriage, to rules to ensure contraceptive insurance coverage for all who wanted it, and to issuing an executive order to make the promise of the DREAM Act possible for young undocumented immigrants, the White House suddenly found the magic formula that wedded its policy ideas to a political agenda that his re-election campaign could reinforce with more than a billion dollars of advertising and public relations.

The elements of the new dominant Democratic coalition—Millennials, minorities and women--clearly represented a new majority on which Obama could count to support his policy agenda. Obama's campaign policy initiatives were designed to solidify the support of this newer and expanding part of the electorate. They directly confronted the "institutions and interests upon which the old politics rested," both in terms of his Republican opposition and, on occasion, among other parts of the Democratic coalition. He consciously chose to side with single and younger women on the issue of contraception and reproductive rights over the Catholic Church, which was influential not just among Republicans but older, ethnic Democratic voters as well. Similarly, his election year conversion to the cause of gay marriage risked alienating not just white evangelical Republicans, but the more conservative members of his extremely loyal African-American base, especially among the influential clergy in that community. And by making immigration a wedge issue designed to split Hispanic and Asian-Americans away from the Republican Party, even at the risk of offending labor union leaders, the President, unlike his timid approach to the issue during the first term, significantly altered the lines of political conflict from the old order of things.

If there was any doubt that the President was determined to put building his new majority at the center of his campaign efforts, regardless of its potential impact on more traditional Democratic constituencies, they were wiped away by the Obama campaign's decision to move the scheduled remarks of Sandra Fluke to prime time on the final and most important night of the Democratic National Convention. Fluke was a young woman, born on the cusp of the generational shift from Gen X to Millennials, who had made such an articulate case earlier for requiring free contraceptive health care under the rules for ObamaCare that Rush Limbaugh felt compelled to pillory her as a "slut," looking for yet another government handout. Now she was given one of the most important time slots in politics to signal to Obama's new coalition that, while the idea might be offensive to some traditional Catholic Democratic voters, the President was prepared to clear "the political and institutional ground" so that "something fundamentally new could take hold."

But President Obama's switch to confrontational, line-in-the-sand politics was not limited to efforts to reshape his own party. His negotiating tactics toward the Tea Party dominated House GOP after his re-election was a clear indicator of Obama's determination to undertake an analogous effort to also reshape the Republican Party's power structure. He began by forcing Speaker John Boehner to break his own rule and let a bill to raise taxes, albeit only on the wealthy, come to a vote even though a majority of his GOP caucus was not ready to break its vows to always support the anti-tax bedrock principle of Reagan revolution orthodoxy. Using public relations tactics borrowed from the campaign, Obama brought such pressure on obstinate Republicans that Speaker Boehner suggested he was trying to "annihilate the Republican Party," a remark which pretty much captured Skowronek's description of the need for reconstructive presidents to "systematically weaken, perhaps even destroy outright," supporters of the old civic ethos.

After winning the fiscal cliff battle with the lame duck Congress, the President adopted an even harder line with those who took office on January 3, 2013. He refused to even negotiate with Republicans on what spending concessions he might make in return for their votes to raise the debt ceiling as the country approached the borrowing limits Congress had established. Even when Democrats urged him to avoid the confrontation by invoking the Fourteenth Amendment or minting a trillion dollar platinum coin, Obama kept his eye on the task of "weakening, if not completely destroying" the political and institutional infrastructure of the old GOP order. He made it clear he would make sure the country blamed Republicans if they jeopardized the full faith and credit of the United States. He won this second battle in the fight for a new civic ethos without even firing a shot when the newly elected Republicans of the 113th Congress agreed at their first retreat to suspend the debt ceiling BEFORE any votes were taken on their spending priorities.

Contrary to the predictions of many pundits and political poseurs who insisted the country wanted the president to compromise without regard to principle, this new political posture toward his opponents did nothing to jeopardize the President's popularity. According to Pew Research, Obama had a 59 percent to 38 percent personal approval rating just before his second inaugural, which was the highest level since the months following his first swearing in ceremony. Eighty-two percent of the public gave him high marks for "standing up for what he believes in" and 76 percent thought he was a "good communicator." Two-thirds thought he was trustworthy. Just under 60 percent thought he was a strong leader who could get things done.

Meanwhile Obama's efforts to cut the ground out from under the old political order appeared to be having an effect. In the same survey, only about a quarter of the population gave the Republican leaders in Congress a favorable rating and only a third bestowed the same seal of approval on the Republican Party. Unlike public expectations when President Obama first came into office, popular opinion had come to expect, if not fully approve of, the partisan fighting that is a hallmark of reconstructive presidencies. Fully two-thirds of Americans thought the two parties would "bicker and oppose one another more than usual" during 2013. This was especially true among Republicans, only 17 percent of whom thought the year would bring a more bipartisan approach to solving problems.

Obama was clearly conscious of the importance of continuing to mold public opinion even after his re-election campaign was over, even quoting President Lincoln on the subject in an interview with NBC's David Gregory before the president's second inauguration. Historian Doris Kearns Goodwin underlined how all transformative, or in her words "best presidents," mobilized pressure on Congress from the outside in, not just by stroking their egos by schmoozing them in the oval office.

Lincoln's famous statement on the topic of public sentiment was made, however, before he even became president. In one of his debates with Stephen Douglas in 1858, at Ottawa, Illinois in an otherwise unremarkable performance, he said, "With public sentiment, nothing can fail; without it nothing can succeed. Consequently he, who molds public sentiment, goes deeper than he who enacts statutes or pronounces decisions. He makes statutes and decisions possible or impossible to be executed." This linkage between public opinion and the ability to execute a shift in the nation's civic ethos remains central to the success of reconstructive presidents more than 150 years later.

Many Washington pundits thought that since Obama's approval ratings were up after the election, he would need to "expend his political capital" to get anything done. But, transformative presidents hone and use their majority coalition to pursue an agenda built around that coalition's beliefs, not on behalf of compromising with the old regime. The real danger for Obama would be to temporize his beliefs and appear to not be operating in the interests of the members of his coalition. For transformative presidents to maintain their newly established majority coalition, the first commandment has to be to "use it or lose it." As a result of the confrontational political posture Obama took during the re-election campaign and the negotiating tactics he employed against his most diehard opponents immediately afterwards, the President had successfully defined the political and public policy ground on which the fight over the country's civic ethos would take place.

Execution Matters

In the past, President Obama had not integrated the first two Ps of presidential leadership, Politics and Public relations, that are so much a part of campaigning, with the other two P's of presidential leadership—Policy and Performance—that are so critical to the daily task of governing. In fact, in his first term he seemed to at least implicitly embrace the progressive notion that good policy would by itself transform American politics. Having been disabused of that notion by the rise of the Tea Party and the unrelenting hostility of the GOP opposition, Obama clearly embarked upon a new approach in his second term, one which integrated all four Ps of presidential leadership.

He went out of his way to advocate policy positions on issues ranging from gun laws to immigration, and from taxes to climate change, to force confrontations with the old political order that exposed the underlying assumptions behind their ideas and made clear the political costs of continuing to adhere to the dogmas of a former political regime. Even when he engaged in new efforts to meet with Republicans in the Congress he made it clear that he was doing so in order to ensure there was a better understanding of each other's viewpoint, not to engage in the kind of half-a-loaf-from- each-side negotiations he had attempted in his first term. This firm approach began to yield dividends sooner than most people expected. The first few tentative efforts at bipartisan cooperation emerged in the U.S. Senate on issues such as immigration reform, gun control, and even deficit reduction right after he followed up his visits to the Hill to meet with Republicans with the kind of White House schmoozing so many commentators had urged him to undertake.

He also made sure the net outcome of this new approach, unlike his somewhat stumbling performance in the second half of his first term, would match the public's expectations for progress by remaking his White House staff and Cabinet and building a political structure capable of winning the political battles that were sure to follow.

Many of the leading figures in Obama's first term cut their political teeth under President Bill Clinton. Obama's first chief of staff, Rahm Emanuel, and Emanuel's successor, Bill Daley, both made their national reputation during Clinton's presidency. Although the most obvious example of this Clinton heritage in the first term was his appointment of Hillary as Secretary of State, the dependency on this seasoned group of Clinton/Gore operatives extended well down into the second and even third tier of the ranks of Obama staffers during his first term. The presence of this potential fifth column among White House staffers was such that one wag joked that if things got really bad these "Manchurian staffers" would be given a signal and switch simultaneously to Hillary as part of a palace coup. Even though some die-hard Clintonites did leave when the President shifted strategies in 2011, for the most part he was able to convert his staff, despite whatever loyalties they may have had originally, into loyal foot soldiers on behalf of his new approach.

Either because of Obama's additional experience, or because of his growing self-confidence in how he wanted to conduct business in his second term, there was no doubt about the loyalties of those he selected to lead his team in the second term. Obama did back away from picking one of his most loyal foreign policy operatives, Susan Rice, as Secretary of State in the face of unrelenting hostility, despite its lack of being grounded in reality, from Republicans to her selection. Still, his later difficulties in getting even a former GOP Senator, Chuck Hagel, confirmed as Secretary of Defense suggests Obama's political instincts that Rice would be too heavy a lift for confirmation in the polarized Senate was probably correct. Outside of these two powerful Cabinet positions, Obama got who he wanted without much difficulty, even though each of his selections was clearly committed to his unique political agenda.

Two examples further illuminate how carefully Obama calibrated the performance he needed from his leading appointees to be successful in implementing the policy and political agenda of his second term. Jack Lew was so identified with President Clinton that the only job Obama would give the former Director of the Office of Management and Budget (OMB) initially was to run State Department operations for Hillary Clinton. But Lew's genius with numbers and his personal integrity were too great to be ignored and he eventually was returned to his former OMB responsibilities by Obama, and then became the president's third chief of staff in 2012. Lew was then selected by the president to be his Secretary of Treasury for the second term, taking the point position on the most contentious policy debates with the GOP. One of Lew's colleagues summed up just how aligned he was with the president's perspective this way, "[Lew] has serious commitments to traditional causes ... but at the same time believes you need to have a solvent government. It always struck me as the Obama approach." When Obama finally produced his first budget of the new term, its call for modest changes to the nation's entitlement programs in order to address the spending side of the equation, coupled with initiatives to expand early education and invest in infrastructure, perfectly reflected the approach Lew had argued for throughout Obama's first term.

Another Cabinet choice that reflected Obama's new approach was his surprise selection of Sally Jewell, the chief executive of Recreational Equipment Inc. (REI) a purveyor of outdoor gear, to lead the Interior Department. She was both a former oil company engineer and longtime advocate for conservation and outdoor recreation who promised to balance the agency's sometimes conflicting mandates to promote resource development and preserve the nation's natural heritage. Her varied background and pragmatic idealism reflected both the Millennial generation's approach to environmental causes and the President's desire to break free from the more doctrinaire Boomer beliefs and political orientation of key members of his original environmental team, many of them former devotees of Vice President Gore's more ideological approach to environmental concerns. Jewell was easily confirmed to her new job by a U.S. Senate that is normally hopelessly divided on environmental issues.

Rebuilding the Party from the Ground Up

The key to being considered a reconstructive president, however, is not based solely upon whether your administration performs well or advocates policies that become popular, but whether or not all four Ps of presidential leadership are integrated so powerfully that they produce lasting change in the president's party. Skowronek asserts, that the "telltale test of reconstructive leadership is party building." It is NOT simply about "discarding the old party of government [Republicans in this case] in favor of the old party of opposition [Democrats]. It is about bringing new groups to power, about rearranging political alliances, about securing an alternative unanticipated by the prior lines of political conflict. Reconstructive leaders establish a new majority that can be depended upon to support the president's new commitments and priorities."

President Obama's efforts to organize his supporters on behalf of his first term agenda through the auspices of "Organizing for America" (OFA) under the umbrella of the Democratic National Committee (DNC) proved to be an ineffective initial attempt at this particular transformational task. As part of the formal structure of the party, the group was unable to do much more than generate phone calls on behalf of the President's legislative agenda. While it could point to some successes in its lobbying efforts on behalf of the historic Affordable Care Act, the top down nature of its operating philosophy, not to mention its very late launch after the 2008 election, drained the energy and excitement from the effort among many of the President's 2008 grassroots supporters.

Freed from these governing constraints during his re-election campaign, Obama rebuilt his operation into the most powerful ground game ever witnessed in American politics. In 2008, the campaign was able to organize about 1.6 million people who agreed to perform at least one shift of work at the mundane but critical tasks of voter registration and turnout. In 2012, more than 2.2 million volunteers were organized by 32,000 "core team leaders" who reported up to 8,237 "neighborhood team leaders," who in turn were overseen by 2,704 paid full-time campaign field organizers.

This effort enabled the campaign to register 1.8 million new voters and turn out voters who had not participated in the 2010 midterm elections. More than half of non-midterm voters who had voted two weeks before Election Day were Democrats, less than a third were Republicans.

Many of these "sporadic" voters were Millennials who were hard to reach by phone. So, the Obama campaign persuaded seven million people on Facebook to reach out to their friends. Twenty percent of the five million people who got a message inspired by this campaign request did what they were asked to do--either by registering to vote, voting or taking some other action to help the campaign. By the time the campaign was over, Obama had collected 32,313,965 friends on Facebook, roughly sixteen times more than in 2008; the Romney campaign had only about a third as many Facebook friends as Obama, 12,135,972.

Having learned the lessons of his first OFA experience, the President was careful not to simply turn this juggernaut over to the "old" Democratic Party after he was re-elected. On the Friday before his second inauguration, the President's team, led by the First Lady, announced the formation of new organization, Organizing for Action, (maintaining the continuity of the acronym, OFA, first adopted in his initial primary run in 2008) that would be completely separate and independent of the Democratic National Committee. The new OFA's website said its mission would be to "support the legislative agenda we voted on, train the next generation of grassroots organizers and leaders, and organize around local issues in our communities."

Both its name and its focus made it clear that this version of OFA was focused squarely on the President's determination to remake the Democratic Party. Less clear was whether its independent organizational home could be financially sustained and even if it could, what long term impact it would have on the Democratic Party once Obama was not in a position to lead its efforts from the White House. Nevertheless, from its organizational conception to its financial approach, this altered version of OFA was clearly designed to bring new groups to power and to rearrange political alliances.

Still, the question remained whether or not such an independent,

Obama-centric initiative would succeed in remaking the party or just become yet another annoyance to traditional Democratic interest groups and elected officials. Those who don't believe Obama will be a transformative president could argue that by directing his efforts through a non-profit entity driven by social media, the President was abdicating or avoiding his responsibilities to get his hands dirty in the nitty-gritty job of remaking his party. On the other hand, those who believe the context of modern media in which political parties operate today requires a broader and more grassroots-oriented approach to party-building could equally make the case that this version of OFA was perfectly suited to accomplishing the second task of a reconstructive presidency in the 21st Century.

That debate won't be settled quickly. Some evidence of the President's success in transforming the Democratic Party will be found in how unified Democrats in Congress are in supporting the president's second term agenda. Another data point will be how many of those Democrats who follow the President's lead are re-elected in the 2014 mid-term elections. But history's final verdict won't be rendered until after the 2016 election, or perhaps even later. If a Democrat who follows in Obama's path is nominated and elected president, then the odds are such a "third term" would give Obama the right to be judged favorably on his efforts to remake the Democratic Party in his coalition's image. However, if the results of the 2016 election are considered to be a repudiation of President Obama, then history is unlikely to render a positive verdict on his novel approach to party building.

Much of Obama's efforts, from OFA to public campaigning for his agenda, can be considered attempts to rearrange institutional relationships in the party and give new interests in his coalition of Millennials, minorities and women a secure grip on power. If successful they would help Obama meet the first two of Skowronek's four criteria for considering a president to have successfully reconstructed or transformed the nation's politics.

However, the final two criteria are much more likely to determine the public's immediate judgment on how successful Obama's presidency was by the time it is over. Both of these criteria--durably recasting government's priorities and making a set of "legitimating ideas" the new common sense of American politics--are focused on public policy initiatives and the ability of the President to convince Congress to follow his legislative lead. Although it is too early in his presidency to issue a definitive judgment on how successful Obama will be in meeting these two criteria, it is clear that in the long run the policies that made up his second term agenda reflected the desire of his new coalition and therefore represented a real opportunity to durably recast the nation's civic ethos before this decade is over.

CHAPTER SIX:
EMBRACING A MILLENNIAL ERA CIVIC ETHOS

The Millennial Era dawned during the 2008 presidential campaign of Senator Barack Obama whose surprise first place showing in the Iowa caucuses, his eventual nomination, and his subsequent general election victory were spurred by the enthusiastic support for his candidacy among Millennials. But the specific contours of this new era were not fully visible until President Obama described it in his second inaugural address and his 2013 State of the Union speech. On both occasions he provided a definitive portrait of the political era America had entered and the policy implications that flowed from the ascendancy of this new majority coalition.

As part of his effort to reshape the nation's civic ethos—its beliefs about the proper role and function of government---President Obama made it clear, just minutes after he took the oath of office for the second time, that "...preserving our individual freedoms ultimately requires collective action," a classic restatement of the Millennial generation's fundamental beliefs about how to solve the nation's problems. Perhaps the most powerful rhetorical device in his speech was his repetition of the phrase, "We the people," the Constitution's clearest statement on the source of a democracy's ultimate legitimacy, to reinforce his belief in the importance of collective action. "We, the people understand that our country cannot succeed when a shrinking few do very well and a growing many barely make it...We, the people, still believe that every citizen deserves a basic measure of security and dignity...We, the people, still believe that our obligations as Americans are not just to ourselves, but to all posterity." He concluded this ringing call for citizen involvement by linking the phrase to the most fundamental statement of the values that underpin the Declaration of Independence: "We, the people, declare today that the most evident of truths—that all of us are created equal—is the star that guides us still."

The president returned to this theme of the importance of collective action at the conclusion of his State of the Union address. The president told the story of three ordinary citizens sitting in the House gallery who had exhibited extraordinary courage while exercising their civic responsibilities. He emphasized the common bond of citizenship that linked all three into one unbroken chain of faith in a democracy that was "well into our third century as a nation." The title "citizen," he said, "describes what we believe. It captures the enduring idea that this country only works when we accept certain obligations to one another and to future generations." Reprising the words of an earlier civic generation president, John F. Kennedy, that it "is the task of us all" to improve the state of the nation, Obama tasked "us all, as citizens of these United States, to be the authors of the next great chapter in our American story."

It was a speech directed at the next great generation of Americans, Millennials, who overwhelmingly supported not just the fundamental idea of the importance of collective action by individual citizens, but the policy implications of the civic ethos that Obama outlined in his remarks to a divided and distrustful Congress. Ron Brownstein summarized how much of a watershed in American politics the president's State of the Union speech represented. "The most striking aspect of Obama's remarks was how unreservedly he articulated the views of the coalition that reelected him, and how little need he felt to qualify those views for fear of alienating voters beyond it. There was a confidence bordering on swagger in his call for action on immigration reform, climate change, and gun control—issues that he almost entirely sublimated through his first term—and his unwavering defense of collective action through government."

All three of the divisive social issues that Brownstein cited were ones that had switched from being wedge issues Republicans had used in previous decades to put Democrats on the defensive to having exactly the opposite political impact because of the increasing presence in the electorate of Millennials and the other major components of the new majority Democratic coalition. Whether it was gun control or gay marriage or immigration the formerly minority viewpoint held by Millennials had become the nation's majority point of view in the course of just a few short years.

Nor were the president's remarks an unplanned assault on the existing political forces arrayed against him. "They [Millennials] are the leading edge of where the country is headed ideologically as well as demographically," one senior White House aide said. "By insisting that entitlement spending on the old must face some limits to prevent it from crowding out investment in the young; by framing climate change as a generational challenge; by pledging to provide young people with more training and to confront rising college costs; and by closing with a paean to citizenship that reflected their civic impulses," as Brownstein also pointed out , Obama repeatedly and consistently spoke over the heads of Congress, a body which contained no Millennials, to the Democratic coalition that had made his victory possible.

The tension between individual liberty and community cohesion has been a part of America's political DNA since its founding. It's the reason Bill Clinton added the word "community" to the New Democrat brand when the words "opportunity and responsibility" struck early audiences as sounding too conservative or Republican. But that appeal, even though it was successful in the 1990's, was not designed to undo the political alignment and policy constraints of its time. What Obama was preaching was a much more direct assault on the country's fundamental beliefs about the role of government. With the emergence of a civic generation, Millennials, Obama realized the center of America's public policy consensus was shifting away from a focus on individual rights toward solutions that benefit the entire community.

Building a New Civic Ethos, Issue by Issue

Evidence for this change in political momentum can be found in the debates that swirled around the Obama administration's policy initiatives. The adoption of ObamaCare in 2010 and its acceptance by the Supreme Court is the most prominent, and possibly the most historically important, example of this change in public sentiment. Even though ObamaCare continued to be an issue that sharply separated Republicans from Democrats, it retained overwhelming support among key elements of the majority coalition, especially Millennials and minorities.

The debate over immigration reform also revealed the impact of Millennials on the nation's civic ethos. One out of five Millennials have an immigrant parent, making the need to bring those who came here illegally into the mainstream of American life not just a political imperative for those seeking to attract their votes, but a critical way to connect with the generation at an emotional level. Seventy-eight percent of Millennials, the highest level of support among all generations, believe people who came here "illegally," should be allowed to stay. Millennials also expressed the highest levels of support for providing a path to citizenship (44%) or granting permanent residency (31%) to undocumented immigrants.

Immigration has always been a difficult issue for America to deal with. The debate has eventually been resolved on the side of a more inclusive policy when a rising tide of recent immigrants' children make their presence felt in the electorate, only to resurface when that electoral imperative subsides.

In response to the increased presence of Irish and German Catholics, the Order of the Star Spangled Banner and a third party associated with it, the Know Nothing Party, won 51 House seats in 1854, while its presidential candidate got eight electoral votes in 1856. But after the Civil War, in which many of these immigrants and/or their children fought bravely for the Union, America once again became a more welcoming place for immigrants, at least those from Europe.

When an even larger wave of immigrants, Catholics and Jews from eastern and southern Europe, engulfed the United States at the turn of the 20th century, the political response was the 1924 passage of a law setting low yearly quotas on immigration from those areas as well as Asia. However, the rising power of the GI generation, many of whom were children of the earlier wave of 20th century immigrants, eventually caused the 1924 quotas to be abolished in the Immigration and Nationalization Law of 1965, signed by a member of their generation, Lyndon Johnson.

The 2013 bipartisan consensus in the U.S. Senate that came together on immigration reform is a reflection of the changes underway in the nation's civic ethos. That compromise includes requirements for dealing with border security and a legal path to eventual citizenship for undocumented immigrants. In keeping with the times, its provisions lean more heavily to protecting the rights of the community than they do to addressing the problems of undocumented immigrants and their families. The unprecedented movement toward passing immigration reform legislation after years of stalemate is a direct result of the recognition by those on both sides of the political aisle, that a new civic ethos, driven by Millennials, is emerging and must be accommodated.

Immigration is just one example of how Millennials' strong beliefs in inclusion and equality are remaking American society. Millennials have also led a major shift on attitudes toward gay marriage. Between 2001 and 2013, the country moved from being opposed to gay marriage by a 57 percent to 35 percent margin to support for it by a 49 percent to 44 percent. Much of this shift was caused by its overwhelming support among Millennials, 70 percent of whom were in favor of allowing gays to marry. At the same time, a consensus in favor of inclusion and equality continued to build within the U.S. Senate, where only two Democrats hesitated to express their support for gay marriage and Republicans found their ranks splitting over the issue.

Millennial beliefs on other previously divisive social issues have also caused the debate over them to become, if not less contentious, at least more predictable, leaning toward Millennials' preference for tolerance of individual behavior within the context of community rules and guidelines.

For example, two-thirds of Millennials now support legalizing marijuana , forming the basis for a national majority in favor of the idea in 2013. Just as the rising clout of the GI generation spurred the repeal of prohibition eight decades ago, the rise of another civic generation, Millennials, will lead to a lessening of penalties and community approbation for the use of a previously banned substance in the years to come.

Millennials have a more nuanced approach to abortion than older generations, something that is well-captured in the movie Juno.

The leading character recoils at the thought of having an abortion when she learns fetuses "have fingernails." She decides to continue her pregnancy, relying on the support of her family to help her with the challenges of single motherhood. Still, the movie makes it clear that she believes that the choice to have a child should remain with the mother and not with male authority figures. Reflecting this sentiment, 68 percent of Millennials oppose overturning the *Roe v. Wade* Supreme Court decision that established the nation's current policy on abortion. Only Baby Boomers equaled this level of support for a decision many of them had fought so hard to protect. Yet 62 percent of Millennials thought abortion was "not that important" an issue, while only 51 percent of Baby Boomers were equally indifferent. As the presence of Millennials in the electorate grows, a middle ground approach balancing individual rights with community cohesion by neither completely prohibiting abortions nor leaving the procedure without some constraints will likely become the consensus position within U.S. politics.

On another emotional issue, the lifelong desire of Millennials for security in an unsafe world will lead to greater restrictions on gun ownership. Pew's basic gun-control question asks respondents if it's more important "to protect the right of Americans to own guns or to control gun ownership." In a mid-January 2013 survey—fielded a month after the Newtown shootings—a 51 percent to 45 percent majority favored emphasizing control on gun ownership rather than protecting the right to own guns. Two years earlier, a 49 percent to 46 percent plurality took exactly the opposite positions.

It is the rise of the Obama Democratic coalition that underpins this new majority support for gun control . The majority of women, Millennials, African-Americans, Hispanics, and college graduates, as well as those who lived in urban and suburban areas and those in the Northeast and West, all support controlling gun ownership over protecting gun owners' rights. As in the 2012 election, these supporters are opposed by a coalition of males, whites, those with incomplete college education, and rural residents, the majorities of whom prefer to protect gun owners' rights.

With the continued emergence of Millennials and the other components of the Democratic coalition, the nation's evolving civic ethos will lead to increased restrictions on gun ownership within the context of the Second Amendment.

On all of these social issues, the continuing influence of Millennials, not just in the electorate but, over the next few decades, as office holders, will transform the United States into a more tolerant and more inclusive nation.

Millennials' Economic Future Lies Ahead

Even as it becomes easier to find consensus on previously divisive social issues, fundamental disagreements on economic and fiscal policy will continue to be a source of confrontation across partisan and coalitional lines for some time to come. Republicans believe that the American economy will be unleashed by freeing it from burdensome regulations and limiting the amount of money diverted to the public sector through taxes, especially on wealthy and corporate "job creators." Democrats have a different viewpoint, believing that government regulation of the economy is necessary to protect the public from "externalities," or costs such as air and water pollution that are not accounted for in the private sector and from the speculative investment practices that preceded both the Great Depression and the Great Recession. Democrats also believe in a more progressive tax system to produce a more egalitarian nation. Which side wins this debate will depend, as it has in the past, on the electorate's perceptions of the performance of the economy under each regime and the lessons each new generation learns as it grows up in vastly different economic circumstances.

For example, members of the Lost Generation, born as the 19th century was ending, experienced economic catastrophe when the Great Depression hit before there were government programs to mitigate the damages. The maternal grandfather of one of the co-authors of this book (Mike Hais) lost his savings when all four banks in his Iowa town collapsed during the Great Depression. He had believed that spreading his money to several banks would protect him. It did not, and there was not yet an FDIC to reimburse his losses. To feed his family, he bootlegged along the Mississippi River in the waning days of Prohibition. When the economy improved, he was able to support himself and his family with a scrap metal business, but he never could accumulate much for his retirement. He ended his days in a dingy room at what was charitably called a "retirement hotel." He got no more than a pittance in Social Security and died a year after Medicare was enacted. In spite of all this, like many others in his individualistic Lost generation who had experienced the economic boom times of the Roaring 20s, he was a lifelong Republican.

By contrast, his children, members of the GI Generation, despite growing up during the Great Depression and coming of age in World War II, enjoyed a rising economy during their family formation years, easily educated their children, were able to save some money and took full advantage of Social Security and Medicare in their retirement years. Like most others in the group-oriented GI generation, they were loyal Democrats, and their generation became the backbone of support for the New Deal.

A similar divide exists today. The oldest members of Generation X experienced the Wall Street driven boom times of the 1980's as they grew up and became the most devoted followers of Ronald Reagan's approach to limiting government's involvement in the economy when they became old enough to vote. Even after their net worth plummeted, when the value of their houses collapsed during the Great Recession, those older Gen-X'ers clung to their Republican loyalties in the voting booth.

Millennials, by contrast, retain a relentless optimism about their economic future even as they face very difficult economic challenges in their early years. Among those with a college degree, only one-half are employed full time and nearly half are employed in jobs that do not require a college degree. The average wage for those who got their first job in 2009-2011 was $27,000 a year, 10 percent lower than those who entered the workforce two years earlier. Lisa Kahn, a labor economist at the Yale School of Management, found in her study of the effects of the 1981-82 recession that the higher the unemployment rate upon graduation, the less graduates earned right out of school; and those workers never really caught up. "The effects were still present 15 or 20 years later," she said. Her comparisons with today's recent graduates suggest the initial wage losses were comparable, and the trend looks set to repeat itself.

Given these different economic experiences, it is not surprising that Millennials are in favor of a much more activist approach to governmental economic policy while older voters, including members of Generation X, are more likely to subscribe to the economic theories of Republicans. A 2011 Pew survey indicated that 51 percent of Millennials believed that, "government regulation of business is necessary to protect the public interest", while only 43 percent indicated that "government regulation of business often times does more harm than good." Voters over thirty were split equally between the two choices (46% each). The same survey found that 54 percent of Millennials preferred a bigger government providing more services rather than a "smaller government with fewer services" (39%). The percentages were exactly reversed among those over thirty.

These generational political disagreements have for the most part led to legislative stalemate on any major economic initiative during Obama's time in office. After the passage of the stimulus package in 2009, the Democratic approach of investing in education, research and infrastructure has been stymied by Republican desires to focus on cutting spending as the nation careened from one congressionally created fiscal crisis to another. Despite the rise of a new Millennial majority coalition nationally, this policy gridlock is likely to continue in Congress for the rest of Obama's time in office.

Neil Howe, the co-author of Generations, believes the financial crisis that will result from failure to deal with the nation's deficits will lead to an "economic winter," far worse than the effects of the Great Recession. Only when the crisis reaches its highpoint does he believe that the political and generational forces will be aligned to deal dramatically and swiftly with the country's economic difficulties.

Others have a more sanguine attitude toward the nation's economy that, even without government action, might provide a firm basis for Millennials' relentless optimism about their economic future. In a private report to his subscribers, the founder of Veritas Economic Analysis, LLC, Robert F. DeLucia, described a number of "positive structural forces underway that have the potential to transform the economy over the next two to three years." His data suggests that the three most significant and positive megatrends are a resurgence of domestic manufacturing, export trade, and domestic oil and gas production. The last one undergirds the first two trends and may be the most significant shift in the American economy Millennials will experience during their lifetime.

DeLucia points out that the transformation of domestic energy production in the United States means that the country will once again become the leading oil and gas producer in the world by the time all Millennials are eligible to vote in 2020. The country will also be the lowest cost producer of energy, enabling it to become a major exporter of both natural gas and petroleum products and to achieve the long dreamed of goal of 100% energy sufficiency within this decade.

In his 2013 State of the Union speech, President Obama reprised some of his campaign lines that summarized how much this change in energy production has already meant for the country. "We produce more oil at home than we have in 15 years. We have doubled the distance our cars will go on a gallon of gas and the amount of renewable energy we generate from sources like wind and solar, with tens of thousands of good, American jobs to show for it. We produce more natural gas than ever before and nearly everyone's energy bill is lower because of it. And over the last four years, our emissions of the dangerous carbon pollution that threatens our planet have actually fallen."

In selecting, Ernest Moniz, a physics professor at the Massachusetts Institute of Technology, to be his new Secretary of Energy, President Obama signaled he was interested in finding the type of win-win solutions on energy policy that Millennials prefer in resolving almost any dispute. At his Senate confirmation hearing, Moniz praised the U.S. natural gas "revolution" brought about by widespread use of fracking and said it must continue. At the same time, he also promoted the transition to a "low-carbon" economy, indicating his Energy Department would continue to invest in solar, wind and other green sources.

Mimicking DeLucia's analysis, Moniz told the Senate Energy Committee that the natural gas "revolution" has led to reduced emissions of carbon dioxide and other gases that cause global warming, as well as a dramatic expansion of manufacturing and job creation. In another indication that the Millennial approach to resolving yet another heated issue from the previous political era was likely to prevail, Moniz's testimony won bi-partisan praise from the committee. If Moniz's and DeLucia's predictions turn out to be right, the return of a "stronger and healthier American economy in 2014-2015" will help solidify the new Millennial majority coalition's support for the Democratic approach to economic policy.

Creating a Better Economic Life Style

Regardless of whether DeLucia or Neil Howe turns out to be right about the country's economic future, there are other forces at work, driven by Millennial lifestyles, that are transforming the fundamentals of America's economy.

Unlike Generation X, Millennials are not interested in striking a balance between work and family life. Instead, their blurring of gender roles and facility in using digital technologies will begin to erase the lines between the two activities. Millennial families will work as much from home as "at work" and share child rearing responsibilities based upon whose work responsibilities require which partner to be away from the house during the day.

The initial impact of these accelerating trends is already visible. Between 2000 and 2010 working at home and not traveling to a job grew at faster rate than any other mode of "going to work." In that decade, the country added some 1.7 million telecommuters, almost twice the increase over those taking public transit, 900,000.

As demographer Joel Kotkin points out , this was even truer in areas where high technology is a major economic factor. Between 2005 and 2009, Silicon Valley's workforce grew by less than 10 percent but the telecommuting population there increased by almost 130 percent. Tech-oriented places like Austin, Portland, Denver, San Diego, San Francisco and Seattle all rank among the cities with the highest percentage of people working at home. A survey by the Information Technology Association of America found that 36 percent of respondents would choose telecommuting over a pay raise, suggesting that these trends will accelerate, especially as tech savvy Millennials continue to increase their presence in America's work force. By 2016, the number of regular telecommuters in the U.S. is expected to reach 4.9 million, a 69 percent increase from the current level.

The impact on America's energy consumption from this shift in where Americans work will be dramatic. A study by Global Workplace Analytics suggested that, if half of Americans worked from home, it would reduce carbon emissions by over 51 million metric tons a year—the equivalent of taking all of greater New York's commuters off the road. Eliminating traffic jams would save almost 3 billion gallons of gas a year and cut greenhouse gas emissions by another 26 million tons. Additional carbon footprint savings would come from reduced office energy consumption, roadway repairs, urban heating, office construction, and business travel.

Furthermore, despite what Yahoo's Generation X CEO, Marissa Meyer, who ordered all of her workers to show up every day at the office, might think, workers who don't spend up to two hours per day driving to and from work are much more productive than those who experience that psychologically draining experience, only to arrive at an office with all the foibles and inefficiencies portrayed in the sitcom, *The Office*. Representatives of Corporate Voices for Working Families, a national business organization whose member companies use workplace flexibility policies, told the U.S Senate that such work arrangements, for both salaried and hourly employees, contribute to more productive work environments, increased employee loyalty, reduced stress, and as a result, increased profitability and global competitiveness. The desire of Millennials to work in such environments will make work an even more productive and less energy consuming activity in the future.

Former Federal Communications Commission Chairman Reed Hundt and National Broadband Plan Director, Blair Levin, point out in their e-book, The Politics of Abundance, another advantage of using Internet technologies. Such services are inherently more capable of customization and therefore more cost efficient, inevitably resulting in lower prices, more consumer choices or both. In the Millennial era, this economic axiom will impact services provided by government and the health care system as well, making both less costly and more effective, thereby lessening the impact of two of the more severe drags on the country's economic productivity.

The result of all of these changes in the economic fundamentals of the American economy should be a growth rate that significantly reduces the level of the country's long term debt to GDP (Gross Domestic Product) ratio, the issue at the heart of Washington's never ending contentious debates over fiscal policy. And as the country's finances improve, finding a solution to the challenge of paying for Baby Boomer's retirement benefits should be easier to do without forcing younger generations to sacrifice their own economic future.

Toward a Millennial Majority Civic Ethos

The Obama administration's first budget after the president's re-election sent the first waves of this potential sea change in America's civic ethos across Washington, D.C., causing predictable ripples in the power center ponds along K Street. The president's proposal to use a "chained CPI" (Consumer Price Index) approach in calculating cost of benefit increases for Social Security recipients (that is, changing the way the index is calculated to better reflect individual's actual buying behavior), thereby lowering payments to future recipients, provoked outrage among members of the Silent generation on both sides of the aisle. But the president was no more speaking to these entrenched interests with his budget message than he was during his State of the Union address.

Instead, his budget proposals were designed to begin to shift the nation's spending priorities to align with the new Millennial majority coalition. The Urban Institute calculates that the federal government currently spends seven dollars on senior citizens for every dollar it spends on younger people. The president's proposals to invest in preschool education, increase college aid, establish an infrastructure bank, expand mental health services for youth and families, and spend billions for summer and full time work for low income youth begin to reverse those priorities. Simon Rosenberg, the head of the DC based think tank, NDN, highlighted the political significance of the president's new budget approach. "Obama is ahead of the party on the future of the coalition."

Matt Segal, the co-founder of OurTime.org, a Millennial advocacy group, captured the opinion of his generation on how Obama's budget helped to meet the needs of everyone in a more balanced way. "We see them [entitlement programs] as being vital, but we also want long-term solvency and realize there is going to be a tremendous tax burden on us if they are not reformed. When the Far Left [says everything] is off the table, that's the same strident conversation that you see from the Tea Party."

Beyond a shift in how the government spends its money and on whom, the power of the Millennial generation will force even more dramatic changes in our system of government. Its belief in collective, direct action at the local level will provide the fuel for a rebirth of civic life in America that may be hard to imagine today.

Millennials are the most service oriented generation in America. The share of college graduates who believe their community is more important than their job doubled between 1982 when Gen Xers were asked the question and 2008 when Millennials answered. This emphasis on community represents the single largest shift in basic values between the two generations. Similarly, 70 percent of entering freshmen in 2009 said it was "essential or very important to help people in need," the highest level since 1970. Millennials, true to their pragmatically idealistic approach to the world's challenges, translate this belief into action. Among those starting college in 2009, 93 percent had done community service in high school, and about half (48%) expected to do so in college as well. Furthermore, this type of locally based, direct action was being undertaken in order to address not just the community's but the nation's challenges. In fact, 85 percent of college-age Millennials considers voluntary community service an effective way to solve the nation's problems.

As a result of these beliefs, Millennials will provide political support for policies that establish national guidelines on a range of individual behaviors. The responsibility for adhering to these guidelines, just as in the case of ObamaCare, will rest with the individual, not the national government. The state's role will be to facilitate the implementation of these guidelines by encouraging the growth of networks of supportive organizations at the community level.

A good example of this approach was President Obama's approach to expanding preschool opportunities throughout the country. He proposed that the effort be funded by increasing the tax on a "bad" behavior, smoking, and using the funds not to open federal pre-schools but to encourage states to create them for their youngest and most needy children. Similarly, he proposed doing something about the high cost of college education by establishing a $1 billion competitive grant program, analogous to his successful Race to the Top competition for K-12 education, to reward states that pledge to lower tuition.

Millennials will play a leading role in a transformation of the civic landscape of America, just as their GI generation forbearers created Kiwanis, Elks, and Rotary clubs in their day. According to the National Conference on Citizenship, this increased civic engagement will also improve the economic trajectory in communities throughout the country.

The institution-building instincts of the Millennial Generation will not only provide a new spurt of civic and economic energy in America, but it will also lessen the current levels of mistrust Americans have in their government. Already, Millennials are the generation most likely to express their support for the nation's governmental institutions. For example, in a 2011 Pew survey Millennials were far less likely to believe that the government is "wasteful and inefficient" (51%) than either Boomers (76%) or members of the Silent generation (73%).

As a result, America's political and governmental structures will emerge from the current period of division and distrust, reconfigured in fundamental ways that reflect the nation's new consensus on the size and scope of government. This Millennial majority civic ethos will produce a more collective, collaborative, and connected country better able to deal effectively with the challenges of America's future.

CONCLUSION

An array of political commentators ranging across the political spectrum, many of whom we have quoted in this book, have engaged in a vigorous, if not always well informed, debate about the implication of the results of the 2012 election for America's political future. Few of them, however, would disagree with the notion that the United States is now moving through an interesting and momentous time in its history. In this book, we have tried to present our own sense of what that future might hold based upon an examination of previous periods of significant demographic and generational change in American history as well as in-depth survey research.

Those who study generational change call an era like the present one a Fourth Turning, a period when a type of generation labeled a civic generation emerges into young adulthood. The United States is in the midst of the fourth Fourth Turning in its history. Previous ones occurred at the time of the American Revolution, the Civil War, and the Great Depression. They begin with a period of rancorous questioning of the very fundamentals of the nation's societal, political, and governmental arrangements--a time of Fear, Uncertainty, and Doubt. They end with the acceptance of a new civic ethos, a consensus on the proper role and function of government. In between, the country experiences an upheaval of society that, in the words of William Strauss and Neil Howe, the founders of modern generational theory, "shakes a society to its roots, transforms its institutions, redirects its purposes, and marks its people (and its generations) for life."

The Revolutionary War Fourth Turning culminated with the creation of the United States itself and the ratification of the Constitution under which the nation is still governed. Under the guidance of Abraham Lincoln and his newly created Republican Party, the Civil War Fourth Turning produced the end of slavery and the recognition of federal supremacy over state and local law and custom. Led by Franklin Roosevelt and the Democratic Party, the Great Depression Fourth Turning responded to the exigencies of industrialization with the assumption of a vastly expanded role for the federal government in stabilizing the nation's economy and at least minimally protecting the living standards of its citizens.

History tells us such eras can end in triumph or tragedy or a bit of both, depending on the wisdom of those entrusted with guiding the nation through such treacherous times. Although it is still too early to forecast exactly how the present Fourth Turning will end and what America's new civic ethos will look like, it is important for those in charge of shaping our nation's destiny today to recognize their place in political time and the role they will need to play in ensuring America's future success. This is not a time for timidity or temporizing. Once the tensions of this turning are resolved, a new America will be born, for good or for ill, and the opportunity to reshape it will not appear again for decades.

We believe a careful examination of public attitudes, current political coalitions, as well as American history, provides a clear sense of where events are taking the country. Just as in the Great Depression Fourth Turning, the Democratic Party seems in a better position than the Republican Party to determine the resolution of the current conflict and shape America's new civic ethos. During the past decade, the Democrats have assembled a majority voter coalition comprised of America's youngest voters, Millennials, minorities, and women that better reflects the demographics, societal arrangements, and economic structure of a changing 21st century United States than the GOP's coalition of seniors, white voters, and men. It was this coalition that elected Barack Obama, the nation's first African-American president, in 2008 and reelected him in 2012, giving him the opportunity to be a transformative president in the manner of Lincoln and FDR.

While partisan politics and electoral results will be of particular interest to inside-the-Beltway pundits over the next decade, most Americans are likely to be more concerned about the content of the nation's next civic ethos and its influence on the public policies that will shape their lives. Historically, the new civic ethos is largely shaped by the characteristics and beliefs of the emerging civic generation.

Today's civic generation, Millennials, is the largest, most educated, ethnically diverse, and gender neutral generation in U.S. history. Similar to previous civic generations, they are group-oriented, optimistic, and accomplished. Like America's last civic cohort, the GI generation, Millennials more strongly favor governmental economic activism, multilateralism in foreign affairs, and greater tolerance of ethnic and lifestyle diversity than older generations.

The behavior and attitudes of Millennials also suggests that the new civic ethos will not be a carbon copy of the GI generation's Depression era civic ethos that built a centralized federal bureaucracy to deal with America's domestic and international concerns. Instead, the Millennial era civic ethos is likely to leverage individual action at the local level to implement national mandates that are enacted to resolve debates about how best to meet the challenges the nation faces and will face in the 21st century.

Of course, none of this is written in stone. The Democrats, Barack Obama, and his successor may make fatal mistakes that could cost them their opportunity to be the dominant force in U.S. elections and politics. The Republicans could develop a message that permits them to connect more effectively with a 21st century America than they have so far. Critical events may push the Millennial generation toward unexpected political attitudes and behaviors.

All of these things *could happen*, but based on what *has happened historically* and so far in this century, the Millennial era is likely to be one in which the Democratic Party, backed by its majority voting coalition, dominates American national elections and shapes a new civic ethos that reflects the group-oriented, tolerant attitudes of its Millennial generation supporters.

For this new civic ethos to develop soon enough to assure America's continued success, older generations will need to find ways to embrace the vision and values of the country's largest, most unified, and youngest adult generation or get out of its way and let

Millennials govern. We hope that this book and its insights will, in some small way, help accelerate that process so that this current chapter in the nation's story ends in the Millennials' and America's triumph.

Epilogue

Two years after we published this book, which predicted that the United States was entering an era when the values and beliefs of the Millennial generation would increasingly come to dominate American politics, a series of remarkable events took place over ten days in June, 2015 signaling that this new era was underway. It all began with the horrific shooting of nine innocent African-American churchgoers in Charleston, South Carolina and culminated in an eloquent eulogy given by President Barack Obama extolling the grace of those worshipers, and of God. What took place within that remarkably short time span made it clear that America had shifted, mysteriously and without advanced warning, toward increased tolerance, inclusivity, and confidence, embodying three key traits of the increasingly omnipresent Millennial generation. While all that happened during those memorable ten days seemed to amaze, and even shock, many observers, those events were, in fact, another indication of trends that we have been documenting since 2008.

As we described in Millennial Momentum (published in 2011), the generation's unique way of approaching the nation's challenges has already begun to form the basis for a new civic ethos that increasingly will come to characterize American government and politics during the rest of this decade when all 95 million members of the generation will have become adults. The cohort's demographic dominance is an inexorable force increasing the chances that the startling changes the country witnessed in the span of less than two weeks are just a foretaste of what America will be like for decades to come.

The first unexpected event suggesting that something different was happening occurred when the families of those slain by a young hate-filled white man forgave him based on their deep religious beliefs. In a courtroom in Charleston the thoughts of Vaclav Havel, the charismatic leader of Czechoslovakia's Velvet Revolution, were accurately, if unknowingly, reflected in the anguished testimonies of the victims' families. "Those who have for many years engaged in a violent and bloody vengefulness against their opponents are now afraid of us. They should rest easy. We are not like them," Havel said at the moment of his triumph over Communism. Similarly, the black families forswore revenge on those who had oppressed their race for generations in order to lay the foundation for a national reconciliation that reached far beyond the Deep South. Their reactions were so unlike the polarizing behavior that has come to characterize American politics that the country stopped and took notice.

The families' courage and grace was followed by an equally unexpected statement from the Republican Indian-American, female Governor of South Carolina, Nikki Haley. Her more timid colleagues, including the state's African-American Republican U.S. Senator, Tim Scott, suggested that discussing the issue of removing the most hated symbol of state's rights and segregation, the Confederate battle flag, from its honored place on the State Capitol grounds might better wait until after the victims had been buried. The Governor instead urged the state's legislature to immediately consider its removal. That step began a badly needed process of healing and reconciliation. But, remarkable as Governor Haley's words were, nothing could better symbolize the generational importance of what was occurring than the remarks of two white Southerners with impeccable "Old South" lineage.

In response to the Governor's comments, Republican State Senator Paul Thurmond, explained why he would vote to remove the flag. "Our ancestors were literally fighting to keep human beings as slaves, and to continue the unimaginable acts that occur when someone is held against their will. I am not proud of this heritage." This from the son of Strom Thurmond, the former South Carolina governor and U. S. Senator, a segregationist candidate for president in 1948 and leader of efforts to defy the nation's civil rights laws in the 1960's, that included raising the Confederate flag above state capitols across the South as a symbol of that defiance.

Equally remarkable was the statement of Reverend Robert

Wright Lee IV, a descendant of Confederate general Robert E. Lee and a scion of an old aristocratic Virginia family. A 22 year old Millennial, Lee is a pastor in the Cooperative Baptist Fellowship, a group that has broken with the conservative Southern Baptist Convention on issues such as women in the pulpit. When asked what he would say if he had an opportunity to speak with the accused murderer, Reverend Lee replied that he would tell him, "You crucified Jesus yet again on the cross of white supremacy."

Within weeks of the Governor's call for its removal, following an overwhelming vote in both houses of the legislature, South Carolina state troopers, led by an African-American officer lowered the Confederate battle flag from the Capitol grounds and dismantled the flag pole from which it had flown for over fifty years. One hundred and fifty years and two months after Lee surrendered at Appomattox, effectively ending the Civil War, the flag was placed where it belonged: in a historical museum. There it serves as a relic from America's past, not a symbol of its future.

The outcome of the debate over the flag was just one of a series of transformative events that swept the country in what many observers called the most historic week of the Obama presidency. On the Monday following the murders, the U.S. Supreme Court, in the case of The Texas Department of Housing and Community Affairs v. Inclusive Communities Project, surprised liberals and conservatives alike by upholding the doctrine of disparate impact as a way to measure violations of the nation's Fair Housing Act. So sure were liberals that the Court would instead begin to require proof of an overt intention to discriminate that they had quietly pushed for settling two earlier cases, expecting the Court to knock out the legal underpinnings for much of the jurisprudence surrounding the country's anti-discrimination laws. Instead, the Court made it clear that statistics, and other evidence, can be used to show that decisions and practices may have discriminatory effects without needing to demonstrate direct discriminatory intentions.

As we documented in Millennial Momentum, the Supreme Court, as the only branch of the federal government whose members enjoy lifetime employment, is usually behind the times initially in reflecting and responding to shifts in public opinion as the country moves from one era to another. Most famously, "nine old men", in Franklin Delano Roosevelt's words, struck down much of the initial New Deal legislation as being unconstitutional in the reach and scope that those laws gave the federal government to interfere in the operation of the nation's economy. But in FDR's second term, having clear evidence from the President's landslide victory in 1936 of where popular opinion stood on these issues, the Court had a change of heart and found no reason to doubt the constitutionality of Social Security or the Wagner Act's rules for collective bargaining, or for that matter any of the myriad New Deal laws that came to its attention in later years. So too, in the Fair Housing decision, a 5-4 majority of the Court decided that the country was best served after all by a vigorous prosecution of those actions leading to the social inequalities that so trouble members of the Millennial generation.

That Supreme Court decision in the Fair Housing case was only a prelude to the 5-4 majority decision making same sex marriage the law of the land, a ruling that was announced on Friday of the same remarkable week. This time it was clear to everyone that the Court was "following the election returns" as Mr. Dooley, Finley Peter Dunne's wise and witty Irish bartender, so famously pointed out more than a century ago. Thanks to the 73 percent of Millennials who support gay marriage, the country's opinion on this controversial topic had shifted at lightning speed from hostility to endorsement during the decade when a majority of the generation became eligible to vote. Even 59 percent of Millennial Republicans favor legalizing gay marriage. Using positive values of love and marriage rather than scolding opponents for their bigotry, allowed the "win-win" Millennial way of making decisions to transform public opinion. In the words of conservative columnist George Will, "whether someone was gay or not became as irrelevant as whether they were right or left handed." All that remained was for the Supreme Court to find a way to embed that new consensus in constitutional principles, which Justice Anthony Kennedy did over the loud and even rude objections of his Boomer conservative colleagues.

A day before the same sex marriage decision was announced; the Court also put its final imprimatur on the validity of the Affordable Care Act, a law that is not only President Obama's signature legislative achievement, but an excellent example of the

Millennial civic ethos that will dominate public policy in the future. As complex as the Act's provisions may be, when taken as a whole, as the Justices did in this particular decision, it sets up a new structure for how government can use its power to shape markets. Millennials decisively favor this type of activist government. An August, 2015 NBC-Wall Street Journal survey indicated that, by nearly two to one, (60% to 37%) the generation believes that government should do more to solve problems, rather than leaving them to businesses and individuals. By contrast, older Americans in the same survey rejected an activist approach by a narrow 46 percent to 50 percent margin.

ObamaCare captures this generational desire for action, but gives government at both the state and federal level a different role to play in solving problems. Its approach is completely different than the New Deal style of problem solving and federal regulation favored by the Greatest Generation, great grandparents of Millennials. For instance, the Affordable Care Act did not, despite the hysterical posturing of its opponents, impose the heavy hand of bureaucracy on health care markets, as it might have done by creating a "public option" for direct federal provision of health care, something many liberals wanted it to do.

In the new Millennial era civic ethos, the roles of the federal government and state governments are separately defined, and the responsibilities for behaving properly are placed squarely on the individual. The Affordable Care Act sets the rules for the nation's health care markets, but doesn't dictate who is allowed to play in the game. It uses the power of the federal government to make the game fairer by offering subsidies to those least able to pay for health insurance. But it also uses the federal government's taxing authority to impose penalties on anyone who seeks to avoid their responsibility to buy health insurance and not play at all. States were seen as the best place for individuals to learn more about their options and to provide solutions tailored to local needs. Some states stepped up to do just that. In others, Republican governors raised ideological objections. This ironically, forced their citizens to interact directly with the federal government the old fashioned way, despite their loud calls for defending states' rights.

All these new roles and responsibilities proved to be confusing at times to the drafters of the detailed legislation, but the Court was correct in deciding by a decisive 6-3 majority that what the Congress intended, a more inclusive and equitable health insurance market, should not be put asunder by judicial intervention based on what was, in effect, a drafting error.

But all of the signs of an emerging consensus didn't just come from a meeting of the judicial and executive minds. In the middle of this most eventful week, Republicans in Congress decided to hand their arch political enemy, President Obama, a victory on trade authority that only one week earlier had been rejected by leaders of the President's own party. The trade negotiating authority he was granted by Congress is the linchpin in Obama's strategy to confront America's largest economic and military rival, China, through economic and diplomatic moves, rather than war. As evidenced by the generation's attitudes toward free trade, this approach is classically Millennial.

A May, 2015 Pew survey found that 69 percent of Millennials say that free trade agreements are "a good thing for the United States," while 56 percent believe that such treaties have helped them personally. Unlike those who represent the economic structures and constituencies of America's past, Millennials have always lived in a time of global competitiveness and are optimistic that they can win any such contest. They lead America in supporting the continued expansion of global trade using the mechanisms of multi-lateral treaties and due process, while providing aid to those who might be hurt by such competition. Whether President Obama, Senator Mitch McConnell, and Speaker John Boehner were listening to the voices of their Millennial constituents when they cut their deal or not, the political fallout from having done so will be much less because of the confidence and optimism Millennials bring to their economic endeavors.

All of these momentous events were only the prelude to the remarkable conclusion to the country's giant step into the Millennial Era, when President Obama addressed a racially-mixed congregation that reflected the diversity and tolerance of the Millennial generation, assembled to mourn the shooting ten days earlier of Reverend

Clementa Pinckney in Charleston's historic Mother Emanuel AME Church.. The President turned to his Christian faith and its notion of grace to explain the actions of the victim's families in forgiving the person who had harmed them, culminating in an act that will be memorialized in every historical account of his presidency. He began singing "Amazing Grace," alone and in acapella style, until the congregation and the organist joined in, inviting everyone in the country to sing along.

He also spoke of the way forward to a better America. He dismissed the typical Boomer generation call for additional conversations about race. Instead the president called for immediate action to address some of the wrongs society has visited upon its most vulnerable and discriminated against minorities. "We talk a lot about race," he said "There's no shortcut. We don't need more talk." Mindful, as he said in a podcast interview earlier in the week, that real progress has been made in America on racial issues, he outlined additional actions that could be taken to improve race relations in both the political and economic spheres. He did not recommend new federal legislation. Instead his suggestions reflected the Millennial generation's belief in thinking globally, but acting locally and individually to solve the big problems confronting the nation. He suggested that employers call back "Jamal and not just Johnny" for job interviews, that local governments work to improve community/police relations, and that states stop trying to restrict voting rights.

History is best seen in a rear view mirror. The passage of time helps clarify which events and decisions turn out to have lasting impact and which do not. Many observers were sure that the 9/11 terrorist attacks would set America on a new course of unity and strength or that the Great Recession would lead to a more populist approach to economic policy. But as important as those events have been in shaping the beliefs of the Millennial Generation, neither led to any new national consensus on how to address the nation's challenges. Instead, even after 9/11 and the Great Recession, the country's politics remained on a continuing course of retribution and resistance, reflecting the deep ideological divisions of America's previously largest generation, Baby Boomers. Consequently, it can't be said with certainty that the sudden alignment of the nation's Supreme Court with the priorities of its chief executive and the willingness of previously hostile political forces to join in an atmosphere of comity and reconciliation will turn out to be as propitious as it appeared at that moment. But there are plenty of signs to suggest that America did become a more tolerant, inclusive, confident and pragmatic country in that amazingly short period of time.

One piece of evidence suggesting this was true occurred two weeks later when President Obama joined five other major countries, including America's most powerful rivals, Russia and China, in signing a treaty in which Iran agreed to dismantle its nuclear weapons program for at least ten years in exchange for lifting the crippling economic sanctions that had brought Iran to the bargaining table. Such an agreement required an American president to take an enormous leap of faith that its friends and adversaries could be counted on to adhere to the deal, and that the country would back such a radical new direction in foreign policy. It represented an unprecedented willingness on the part of the most powerful country on earth to join with other countries, as well as the United Nations Security Council, to reject confrontation and threats of war in favor of a more peaceful approach to dealing with very real threats to global peace.

Depending on how the question was posed to respondents, initial polling on the issue provided conflicting indications about the American public's attitude toward the proposed agreement. One thing was clear, however. Millennials supported the treaty to a significantly greater extent than any other generation. The August, 2015 NBC-Wall Street Journal survey found the Millennial Generation was the only generational cohort in which a clear plurality favored the proposed nuclear arms limitation agreement with Iran (40% in favor,19% opposed, with the remainder uncertain).

These findings are in alignment with previous research on foreign policy matters indicating that the Millennial Generation, whenever possible, favors "win-win" solutions that avoid direct confrontations with America's global opponents. In the longer term, if the deal survives its test of political fire in Congress and is honored by Iran, its framework could become the basis for a Millennial era foreign policy approach that uses economic leverage to restrain belligerent behavior rather than war, on the one hand, or capitulation to would-be bullies on the other.

Despite the many challenges that still confront the country, we believe, as the President suggested in his eulogy to Reverend Pinckney and his parishioners, that as the Millennial Era unfolds, not only will God continue to shed his grace on America, but also that the final lines of the revered patriotic hymn, "America the Beautiful," will become even truer. As America embraces Millennials' values, it will be more completely crowned "with brotherhood from sea to shining sea."

We end our trilogy about Millennials and their impact on American life as confidently as when we started more than seven years ago: with optimism and faith in the power and wisdom of America's next great generation.

REFERENCES

In addition to the hyper-linked articles embedded throughout this book, we found the following books useful in developing our analysis and recommend them for further reading for those who might be interested:

Buffa, D. and Winograd, M. *Taking Control: Politics in the Information Age* (H. Holt: 1996)

Campbell et al., *The American Voter* (Wiley: 1960)

Goldwin, R. A. ed., *100 Years of Emancipation* (Rand McNally & Co.:1964)

Lewis-Beck et al., *The American Voter Revisited* (University of Michigan Press: 2008)

Skowronek, S. *Presidential Leadership in Political Time: Reprise and Reappraisal* (University Press of Kansas: 2010)

Strauss, W. and Howe, N. *Generations: The History of America's Future, 1584 to 2069* (William Morrow & Co.: 1991)

Strauss, W. and Howe, N. *The Fourth Turning* (Broadway Books: 1997)

Trende, S. *The Lost Majority: Why the Future is Up for Grabs—and Who Will Take It (*Palgrave Macmillan: 2012)

Winograd, M. and Hais, M. *Millennial Makeover: MySpace, YouTube and the Future of American Politics* (Rutgers University Press: 2008)

Winograd, M. and Hais, M. *Millennial Momentum: How a New Generation is Remaking America* (Rutgers University Press: 2011)

Author Photo by Aleks Bienkowska

Endnotes

1. The percentage of Americans who are Christian has fallen to about three-quarters... http://www.pewforum.org/2012/10/09/nones-on-the-rise/
2. But, for almost the following six decades, because more traditionally-minded women were hesitant to exercise the suffrage... http://www.ssdan.net/content/voter-turnout
3. By the turn of the next century, employment for pay among married women had risen to 60 percent and among single women to 69 percent. http://www.pbs.org/fmc/book/2work8.htm
4. By 2010 women comprised a majority (54%) of the nation's workforce as well as its electorate. http://www.infoplease.com/ipa/A0104673.html
5. Starting as far back as the 1940s, women have been as likely to attend high school as men. http://www.usnews.com/education/blogs/high-school-notes/2011/06/13/national-high-school-graduation-rates-improve
6. That year, women earned 63 percent of associate's degrees, 58 percent of bachelor's degrees... http://www.nytimes.com/2006/07/09/education/09college.html
7. Although women may have taken better advantage of the change, the entire U.S. population has benefitted from a large scale increase in educational achievement over the past century. http://www.census.gov/hhes/socdemo/education/data/cps/historical/fig2.jpg
8. In 1940, according to the calculations of Ruy Texiera and Alan Abramowitz, 58 percent of employed whites were "working class" (manual workers or farmers). www.brookings.edu/~/media/research/files/papers/2008/4/demographics%20teixeira/04_demographics_teixeira.pdf
9. The pundits' perceptions that economics would override the loyalty to the president and his party of the new components of the Democratic coalition was reinforced by polls... http://www.people-press.org/2012/09/28/youth-engagement-falls-registration-also-declines/
10. Right up to Election Day Republicans and conservatives, believed this "enthusiasm gap" would propel Mitt Romney to the White House. http://www.forbes.com/sites/rickungar/2012/10/08/voter-enthusiasm-gap-the-real-challenge-to-obama-re-election/2/
11. CIRCLE, a non-partisan organization that researches and strives to increase youthful civic participation... http://www.civicyouth.org/at-least-80-electoral-votes-depended-on-youth/
12. Meanwhile, numerous post-election articles described the devastating impact of Mitt Romney's and the GOP's abysmal performance among Hispanics... http://news.yahoo.com/poll-latino-vote-devastated-gop-even-worse-exits-181922111--politics.html

13. Today, at least some Republicans believe that a more traditional Democratic presidential nominee will be easier to defeat in 2016 than the African-American... http://www.economist.com/blogs/democracyinamerica/2012/05/presidential-cartoon

14. The gender gap separating the political attitudes and voting preferences of women and men first emerged...http://www.people-press.org/2012/03/29/the-gender-gap-three-decades-old-as-wide-as-ever/

15. Furthermore, a majority of the first segment of Millennials to vote for president cast ballots for John Kerry... http://elections.nytimes.com/2008/results/president/national-exit-polls.html

16. Never have fewer than 82 percent of African-Americans voted Democratic for president since the 1960s... http://www.thenation.com/article/exclusive-lee-atwaters-infamous-1981-interview-southern-strategy/

17. After the election results were in, Republican pollster, Frank Luntz pointed to the historical parallels between President Obama's and Franklin Delano Roosevelt's re-election... http://poy.time.com/2012/12/19/the-choice/#ixzz2GIW3lXFn

18. All told, political expenditures exceeded $6 billion in 2012. http://www.npr.org/sections/itsallpolitics/2012/11/05/164207894/any-way-you-describe-it-2012-campaign-spending-is-historic

19. In a rare moment of candor, Romney advisor Eric Fehrnstrom said... http://www.nytimes.com/2012/03/22/us/politics/etch-a-sketch-remark-a-rare-misstep-for-romney-adviser.html?_r=0

20. This impression was reinforced by his offer to bet Texas Governor Rick Perry $10,000 to settle a debate disagreement on healthcare policy. http://www.washingtonpost.com/blogs/the-fix/post/mitt-romneys-10000-mistake/2011/12/11/gIQA9aEQpO_blog.html

21. All of these problems with Romney as a messenger were crystallized by the candidate's own words in a video... http://www.motherjones.com/politics/2012/09/full-transcript-mitt-romney-secret-video

22. A Pew survey taken about 10 days before the November election revealed the extent to which these beliefs about Romney had taken hold within the electorate. http://www.people-press.org/2012/10/29/presidential-race-dead-even-romney-maintains-turnout-edge/

23. Demonstrating the accuracy of John F. Kennedy's aphorism that "victory has a thousand fathers, but defeat is an orphan,"... http://www.brainyquote.com/quotes/quotes/j/johnfkenn110295.html

24. . Typical was this comment by Jenny Beth Martin of the Tea Party Patriots: "We wanted someone who would fight for us... http://politicalticker.blogs.cnn.com/2012/11/07/a-day-after-loss-conservatives-point-fingers/

25. From the perspective of some Republican governors, such as Louisiana's Bobby Jindal... http://latino.foxnews.com/latino/politics/2012/11/16/susana-martinez-mitt-romney-comments/

26. Romney didn't improve his image with the public by saying

in his first postelection TV interview that President Obama had won reelection through "targeted gifts" to minorities... http://www.usatoday.com/story/news/politics/2012/11/15/romney-obama-won-with-gifts-to-certain-voters/1706223/

27. By 2012, almost half (47%) of American voters used the Internet as a source for news about the campaign... http://www.people-press.org/2012/11/15/section-4-news-sources-election-night-and-views-of-press-coverage/

28. An October 2012 Google survey of 2,500 Internet users indicated that 64 percent believed that the president's campaign was more adept at social media ... http://www.forbes.com/sites/karstenstrauss/2012/10/09/obama-beats-romney-in-internet-savvy-social-media/

29. In 2012, according to Pew, "the only news of the day comes directly from the Obama campaign itself." http://www.journalism.org/2012/08/15/how-presidential-candidates-use-web-and-social-media/

30. An article by technology writer, Sean Gallagher, with the apt title, "How Team Obama's Tech Efficiency Left Romney IT in [the] Dust,"... http://arstechnica.com/information-technology/2012/11/how-team-obamas-tech-efficiency-left-romney-it-in-dust/

31. As the New Republic's, Noam Scheiber put it, the Romney campaign perceived the electorate from a "best-case" rather than "worst-case" perspective. http://www.newrepublic.com/blog/plank/110597/exclusive-the-polls-made-mitt-romney-think-hed-win

32. These programs were called ORCA, a dig at Obama's Narwhal program. http://www.dailykos.com/story/2012/11/10/1160145/-How-Romney-s-ORCA-was-defeated-by-Obama-s-Narwhal-Dreamcatcher

33. According to Jason Bloomberg, of Zap Think, the possible benefits of ORCA were hindered by the Romney campaign's reliance on best-case scenarios... http://www.devx.com/blog/narwhal-vs.-orca-the-big-data-story-of-the-2012-election.html

34. But ORCA's difficulties went beyond the outcomes expected by its users. http://arstechnica.com/information-technology/2012/11/inside-team-romneys-whale-of-an-it-meltdown/

35. In fact, Narwhal and Dream Catcher were designed to patch flaws in the campaign's IT programs... http://www.dailykos.com/story/2012/11/10/1160145/-How-Romney-s-ORCA-was-defeated-by-Obama-s-Narwhal-Dreamcatcher

36. The Romney campaign was entirely dark on cable TV for two of the campaign's last seven days." http://www.reuters.com/article/2013/01/05/us-usa-politics-cabletv-idUSBRE90406820130105

37. In March 2013, Republican National Committee Chairman, Reince Priebus, announced a detailed plan to rebuild the GOP... http://www.nationalreview.com/corner/343266/reince-priebus-party-growth-and-opportunity-nro-staff

38. As Justin Fox, the Editorial Director of the Harvard Business

Review, pointed out... https://hbr.org/2013/03/the-gop-needs-a-new-product-no.html

39. However, although Reince Priebus spoke of a need to change just about everything in the way the Republican Party operates... http://www.nationalreview.com/corner/343266/reince-priebus-party-growth-and-opportunity-nro-staff

40. Tea Party leader, Jenny Beth Martin, condemned the report... http://www.npr.org/sections/itsallpolitics/2013/03/18/174689113/rnc-chairs-postmortem-report-a-line-in-the-sand-for-divided-gop

41. Rush Limbaugh also vigorously attacked the effort... http://www.rushlimbaugh.com/daily/2013/03/18/the_gop_s_real_problem_is_simple

42. A survey of its readers by Conservative HQ... http://www.conservativehq.com/article/12639-priebus-vs-limbaugh-chq-readers-say-no-contest-rush-wins

43. In a BuzzFeed article about those tech-savvy young Republicans... http://www.buzzfeed.com/zekejmiller/a-new-republican-generation-gets-ready-to-take-ove

44. As the Washington Post's, Chris Cillizza and Sean Sullivan wrote... http://www.washingtonpost.com/news/the-fix/wp/2013/03/18/can-reince-priebus-save-the-republican-party/

45. Citing the research of political scientist Samuel Popkin, Cooper wrote... http://www.nationaljournal.com/politics/why-the-rnc-s-reforms-don-t-solve-the-gop-s-problem-20130318

46. Republican consultant, Mike Murphy, sees this as a likely outcome. http://www.washingtonpost.com/politics/will-the-real-republican-party-please-stand-up/2013/03/17/9f61709c-8f15-11e2-bdea-e32ad90da239_story.html

47. Pew survey researcher, Andrew Kohut, indicates that factional differences within the Republican Party are not as great as some believe. https://www.washingtonpost.com/opinions/the-numbers-prove-it-the-republican-party-is-estranged-from-america/2013/03/22/3050734c-900a-11e2-9abd-e4c5c9dc5e90_story.html

48. During the past decade, through a fortuitous combination of strategic thinking and being in the right place... http://ndn.org/paper/2010/american-electorate-21st-century-poll-presentation

49. Justin Fox, in his Harvard Business Review article that primarily focused on the Republicans' proposed reforms... https://hbr.org/2013/03/the-gop-needs-a-new-product-no.html

50. Recent survey research suggests that at the moment, at least, the Democratic Party coalition is solidifying. http://www.people-press.org/2012/08/23/a-closer-look-at-the-parties-in-2012/

51. This matched the collections and expenditures of the Romney campaign... http://elections.nytimes.com/2012/campaign-finance

52. By contrast the RNC's centralized voter database logged only about half as many interactions... http://techpresident.com/news/23479/

republican-partys-technology-revival-hopes-hinge-more-just-skype

53. . In a post-election article in San Jose's Mercury News, GOP consultant, Kevin Spillane, pointed out... http://www.mercurynews.com/presidentelect/ci_22189775/gop-has-lost-another-key-bloc-silicon-valley

54. Democrats are not taking their current lead in high-tech communication technology for granted... http://techpresident.com/news/23618/tech-arms-race-democratic-national-committee-also-hiring

55. So far, the Democrats' message appears to be connecting with the major components of its emerging coalition... http://www.nationaljournal.com/thenextamerica/politics/opinion-women-minorities-and-millennials-will-determine-america-s-next-civic-ethos-20121001?mrefid=site_search

56. On issues ranging from government economic activism and social welfare to foreign policy and from gun control... http://www.nationaljournal.com/thenextamerica/politics/opinion-obama-s-electoral-coalition-is-now-his-policy-coalition-20130124?mrefid=site_search

57. [to] gay marriage... http://www.people-press.org/2013/03/20/growing-support-for-gay-marriage-changed-minds-and-changing-demographics/

58. [as well as] immigration... http://www.people-press.org/2013/03/28/most-say-illegal-immigrants-should-be-allowed-to-stay-but-citizenship-is-more-divisive/

59. . In a National Journal article published two days after Barack Obama's reelection... http://www.nationaljournal.com/magazine/the-american-electorate-has-changed-and-there-s-no-turning-back-20121108

60. During the 2012 campaign, they argued that the Obama campaign needed to make a "Clintonian pivot"... http://www.wsj.com/articles/SB10000872396390443847404577631150151855674

61. The demographics of the electorate have changed.. http://www.nationaljournal.com/thenextamerica/politics/with-new-support-base-obama-doesn-t-need-right-leaning-whites-anymore-20130201

62. Although they are as likely as older generations to believe that Social Security... http://www.rooseveltcampusnetwork.org/

63. According to Pew Research, Obama had a 59 percent to 38 percent personal approval rating... http://www.people-press.org/2013/01/17/obama-in-strong-position-at-start-of-second-term/

64. Lincoln's famous statement on the topic of public sentiment was made, however, before he even became president. http://quod.lib.umich.edu/j/jala/2629860.0015.204?rgn=main;view=fulltext

65. . For transformative presidents to maintain their newly established majority coalition... http://www.huffingtonpost.com/michael-hais-and-morley-winograd/if-you-dont-use-it-you-lo_b_437387.html

66. One of Lew's colleagues summed up just how aligned he was with the president's perspective this way, "[Lew] has serious

commitments to traditional causes. http://www.newrepublic.com/blog/plank/111780/when-it-comes-worldview-jack-lew-obama-in-coke-bottle-glasses?utm_source=The+New+Republic&utm_campaign=c6a3035385-TNR_Daily_011013

67. Another Cabinet choice that reflected Obama's new approach was his surprise selection of Sally Jewell... http://www.nytimes.com/2013/02/07/us/politics/obama-chooses-rei-executive-to-lead-interior-dept.html?nl=us&emc=edit_cn_20130206&_r=0

68. Freed from these governing constraints during his re-election campaign, Obama rebuilt his operation into the most powerful ground game ever... http://techpresident.com/news/23226/jeremy-bird-future-organizing-america-2012-and-beyond

69. This effort enabled the campaign to register 1.8 million new voters... http://www.huffingtonpost.com/2012/10/24/obama-ground-game-swing-states_n_2009600.html

70. So, the Obama campaign persuaded seven million people on Facebook... http://techpresident.com/news/23202/obamas-targeted-gotv-facebook-reached-5-million-voters-goff-says

71. By the time the campaign was over, Obama had collected 32,313,965 friends on Facebook... http://techpresident.com/news/23178/presidential-campaign-2012-numbers

72. Both its name and its focus made it clear that this version of OFA... https://my.barackobama.com/page/s/organizing-for-action

73. Ron Brownstein summarized how much of a watershed in American politics... http://www.nationaljournal.com/columns/political-connections/courting-the-twenty-somethings-20130214

74. [Millennials] are the leading edge of where the country is headed ideologically as well as demographically... http://www.nationaljournal.com/columns/political-connections/courting-the-twenty-somethings-20130214

75. Seventy-eight percent of Millennials, the highest level of support among all generations, believe people who came here "illegally," should be allowed to stay. http://www.people-press.org/2013/03/28/most-say-illegal-immigrants-should-be-allowed-to-stay-but-citizenship-is-more-divisive/

76. Millennials have [led a shift] on attitudes toward gay marriage. http://features.pewforum.org/same-sex-marriage-attitudes/slide2.php

77. At the same time, a consensus in favor of inclusion and equality... http://www.thenewcivilrightsmovement.com/democratic-us-senator-mark-pryor-im-opposed-to-gay-marriage/politics/2013/04/09/64875

78. For example, two-thirds of Millennials now support legalizing marijuana... http://www.people-press.org/2013/04/04/majority-now-supports-legalizing-marijuana/

79. Only Baby Boomers equaled this level of support for a decision many of them had fought so hard to protect. http://www.pewforum.

org/2013/01/16/roe-v-wade-at-40/

80. Even after their net worth plummeted, [those] older Gen-X'ers clung to their Republican loyalties in the voting booth. www.urban.org/UploadedPDF/412766-Lost-Generations-Wealth-Building-Among-Young-Americans.pdf

81. Millennials, by contrast, retain a relentless optimism about their economic future... http://centerforcollegeaffordability.org/research/studies/underemployment-of-college-graduates/

82. Her comparisons with today's recent graduates suggest the initial wage losses.. http://www.nytimes.com/2013/03/31/magazine/do-millennials-stand-a-chance-in-the-real-world.html

83. A 2011 Pew survey indicated that 51 percent of Millennials believed... http://www.people-press.org/2011/05/04/beyond-red-vs-blue-the-political-typology/

84. At his Senate confirmation hearing, Moniz praised the U.S. natural gas "revolution"... http://www.washingtontimes.com/news/2013/apr/9/obamas-energy-department-nominee-lauds-fracking-re/

85. The initial impact of these accelerating trends is already visible. http://www.newgeography.com/content/002500-major-metropolitan-commuting-trends-2000-2010

86. As demographer Joel Kotkin points out, this was even truer in areas where high technology is a major economic factor. http://www.newgeography.com/content/003082-the-rise-telework-and-what-it-means

87. A survey by the Information Technology Association of America found that 36 percent of respondents... http://www.cnn.com/2007/LIVING/worklife/09/27/cb.work.home.advantage/index.html

88. A study by Global Workplace Analytics suggested that, if half of American... http://globalworkplaceanalytics.com/pros-cons

89. Simon Rosenberg, the head of the DC based think tank, NDN, highlighted... http://www.nationaljournal.com/columns/political-connections/a-new-budget-for-a-new-party-20130411

90. Matt Segal, the cofounder of OurTime.org, a Millennial advocacy group... http://www.nationaljournal.com/columns/political-connections/a-new-budget-for-a-new-party-20130411

91. According to the National Conference on Citizenship... http://ncoc.net/unemployment2

92. For example, in a 2011 Pew survey Millennials were far less likely to believe that the government is "wasteful and inefficient... http://www.people-press.org/2011/11/03/section-7-views-of-government/

Made in the USA
San Bernardino, CA
03 August 2016